LATIN AMERICAN
VEGETARIAN
COOKERY

Rider books also by David Scott

Middle Eastern Vegetarian Cookery
Indonesian Cookery (with Surya Winata)
The Vegan Diet (with Claire Golding)
A Taste of Thailand (with Kristiaan Inwood)
The Penniless Vegetarian
Protein-Rich Vegetarian Cookery

LATIN AMERICAN VEGETARIAN COOKERY

DAVID SCOTT & EVE BLETCHER

Illustrated by Steve Hardstaff

RIDER

LONDON • SYDNEY • AUCKLAND • JOHANNESBURG

First published in 1994

1 3 5 7 9 10 8 6 4 2

Copyright © David Scott 1994
Illustrations © Steve Hardstaff 1994

Published in 1994 by Rider,
an imprint of Ebury Press, Random House,
20 Vauxhall Bridge Road, London SW1V 2SA

Random House Australia (Pty) Limited
20 Alfred Street, Milsons Point, Sydney,
New South Wales 2061, Australia

Random House New Zealand Limited
18 Poland Road, Glenfield,
Auckland 10, New Zealand

Random House South Africa (Pty) Limited
PO Box 337, Bergvlei, South Africa

Random House UK Limited Reg. No. 954009

The paper in this book is acid-free/recycled/chlorine free

A CIP catalogue record for this book
is available from the British Library

ISBN 0-7126-5960-9

Typeset by Textype Typesetters, Cambridge
Printed by Mackays of Chatham plc, Chatham, Kent

Authors' Note

Dishes are generally named in English, followed, where known, by the local name. A few dishes, however, are only given their Spanish name. This is the case where there is no satisfactory English translation or where a dish is well known internationally by its Spanish name.

We have also given, where known, the country of origin of a dish. If the country of origin is omitted, it is either unknown or the dish is common to several Latin American countries.

Acknowledgements

Thank you to Maria Fernandez for her help with Spanish translation, to Gillian Etherington for checking the manuscript, to Nick Spalton for his help in tracing published works on Latin American cookery and to Pilar Carstairs for her checking of the text for authenticity.

Contents

Introduction

Latin American vegetarian cookery is as richly diverse and exciting as the countries of Central and South America themselves. There is, however, an underlying common influence of Spanish and native Indian origin, with the customs of immigrant groups from various parts of Europe and Africa playing a role to a greater or lesser degree in individual countries – the Portuguese and Africans in Brazil, the Italians in Argentina and the Germans in Chile. Climate and geography have also had a most important effect on particular cuisines, and styles tend to overlap where terrain and climate are similar. Latin America is the home of products such as corn, potatoes, tomatoes, chilli peppers, avocados, peanuts, cassava, a variety of beans, sweet potatoes and pineapples. These ingredients, together with foods introduced by European explorers, such as wheat, rice, onions, garlic and dairy products, and tropical fruits from the Caribbean, are the basic ingredients of the various cooking styles.

Peruvian cuisine is influential throughout Latin America and it perhaps reflects best the continent's mixture of cultures. Its culinary traditions are a mix of those of the Quechua Indians (also named after their leader the Inca), of their conquerors, the Spanish, and of the black Africans taken to South America as slaves by the Spanish. Climate adds a further diversifying factor. The narrow coastal plain between the Andes and the Pacific Ocean is dry and desert-like. The wide Andes mountain ranges that occupy most of the country are temperate. Much of this terrain has been terraced and cultivated and the Quechuas are credited with developing many varieties of the staples corn, potatoes and chilli peppers. The inland valleys of the Peruvian Andes are hot, humid, tropical regions where many fruits and vegetables are grown. The dish *causa a la chiclayana* demonstrates the cross-cultural and climatic origins of the region's cooking style. Pieces of baked sweet potato, strips of cheese, slices of fried ripe plantain, corn on the cob and black olives are arranged on a bed of mashed potato. Like this dish, Peruvian food is often predominantly yellow, perhaps a culinary repository of the Inca's worship of the sun.

Bolivian cuisine is very like that of Peru, of which Bolivia was once part. Body-warming soups and stews are popular in this country of high altitude and cold climate. The staple food is the potato, most often served with a spicy sauce or mashed with lemon juice, olive oil and chopped onions.

Mexican cuisine is the other most influential and perhaps best known style of Latin American cooking. Mexico is the most northerly country in Latin America and, like Peru, it has many mountain ranges. Corn, rice, beans and chillies are the country's favourite foods.

Chillies come in a huge variety of shapes, colours and degrees of hotness, and often a simple dish will call for the use of several different types. This is true of dishes from many parts of Latin America. Since we do not have the luxury of such variety, we have simplified the recipes in this book for such dishes and used only the regular chilli pepper, now widely available in vegetable shops and supermarkets.

In Mexico, corn (maize), as elsewhere in Central and South America, is used in many forms. Corn on the cob and corn kernels are used as a grain-cum-vegetable, while cornmeal flour (*masa harina*) is used to make staple foods such as tortillas and tamales. Tortillas, the basis of many dishes, are essentially flat pancakes (sometimes also made with wheat flour or a mixture of wheat and corn flour), but they appear in many forms and sizes and in soft or crunchy textures. They may be used as a plate or a scoop for eating with, or stuffed with a filling and rolled up, or as tacos, tostadas, enchiladas, quesadillas and so on. Corn flour and tortilla dishes are discussed in more detail in the chapter Tortillas, Tortilla Dishes and Breads. Frozen or cling-wrapped, ready-made tortillas are now readily available in the UK from specialist shops and some supermarkets.

Beans are another staple of the Mexican diet and in one form or another they are served at most meals. Sauces (*salsas*) such as *salsa cruda*, a freshly made condiment of chopped tomatoes, onion, chillies and coriander leaves, are also regulars at mealtimes.

The cooking of Belize and Guatamala includes Mexican-style dishes such as tacos and enchiladas, but it has also been influenced by British and German dishes and the Caribbean cooking introduced by banana plantation workers from the West Indies. As one moves south through Nicaragua, Costa Rica, and Panama, the influence of native cuisines becomes more apparent and potatoes along with corn, beans and rice are the staple foods of the region. *Arepa*, consisting of small pan-fried cakes of cornbread, sometimes stuffed with cheese, is a popular dish. Venezuela and Colombia grow a wide range of foods. The mountainous cold areas grow excellent potatoes, while fruits such as avocados and coconuts are found in the tropical lowlands. Food cooked in coconut milk is characteristic of the coastal areas. Rice with coconut and raisins is a typical dish. Both countries also grow some of the best coffee beans in the world. The climates of the high regions seem to bring the best out of the coffee plant.

Brazil is a huge country, stretching from the tropics in the north to the temperate climes of the south, and with a wide ethnic mix. Brazilian food is the most varied in Latin America. It ranges from the predominantly African-influenced cooking of the north, with its spicy colourful dishes cooked in nutty-flavoured palm oil (dende) using ingredients such as coconuts, beans, hot peppers, cashews, almonds, peanuts and manioc, to the Portuguese-style food of the south, where vegetables are appreciated in their own right as well as included in thick soups and stews, and where desserts rich in egg yolks and sugar are still very popular.

Potatoes are cooked in many imaginative ways in Ecuador. They are made into *locro*, a thick potato and cheese soup that is sometimes served with avocado slices. Another popular dish is *llapinga-chos*, fried potato and cheese cakes traditionally served with *salsa de maní*, peanut sauce. Several Spanish dishes were assimilated into the Ecuadorian cuisine, but, as in Peru, the cooking strongly reflects the country's pre-Columbian past.

The countries of Chile, Argentina and Uruguay do not have really distinct cuisines and they are as much influenced by Spanish, Italian and German cooking styles as by local culinary traditions. For instance, *almendrado*, an Italian ice-cream cake with chocolate almond sauce, is popular in Argentina and Chile. Pastries with fruit and caramel fillings are also common and delicious. *Empanadas*, tiny spicy pies, are eaten at all hours of the day, but like most savoury dishes of this region they are usually based around a meat filling. Chile has good soil and the country's farmers grow excellent wine-producing grapes, fruits, Jerusalem artichokes and many types of beans, of which Chilians are very fond.

This is a very brief outline of the culinary roots of Latin American cookery and as you can see they create a complex and rich pattern. It would not be possible to provide anything like a complete coverage of the vegetarian dishes of the area since, apart from the space available, many ingredients required would not be easily obtainable in the UK. Hence we have chosen a range of colourful and exciting dishes that give a representative flavour of the various culinary styles of the area but which are also practical, that is they use available ingredients and well-known cooking methods.

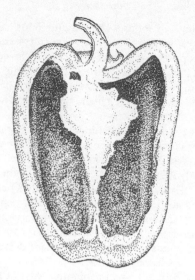

Ingredient Notes

BEANS

Beans, especially black, pinto, red and white kidney beans and chickpeas, are an intrinsic ingredient of many Latin American dishes. If you use dried beans rather than the tinned cooked variety, it is important to cook them properly to avoid indigestion. Beans contain two starches which are difficult to digest if they are not broken down before eating and they need to be soaked and cooked for the correct time before consumption. This particularly applies to kidney beans, which also contain a harmful substance destroyed only by correct cooking.

To Prepare and Cook Dried Beans

Method 1 Weigh out the beans you require (6–8 oz (175–225 g) serves about four people). Pick over and remove any stones and damaged beans, place in a large pan or bowl and for every 8 oz (225 g) beans pour on about 2 pints (1.2 litres) cold water so that the beans are covered. Leave to soak overnight. Then drain and rinse, cover with fresh water, bring to the boil and boil vigorously for 10 minutes. Then lower the heat and allow to simmer, covered, until tender. The average cooking time will be about 1½ hours for most beans. Very old beans will take longer. If water needs to be added during the cooking time, it should always be hot; adding cold water at this stage could make the beans tough. Do not add salt until near the end of the cooking time, otherwise the beans will harden and take longer to cook.

If you forget to leave the beans to soak, then use the following quick-soak method:

Method 2 Weigh out and pick over the beans as above. Then again place them in a large pan and cover with cold water (about 2 pints (1.2 litres) for every 8 oz (225 g) beans). Cover the pan, bring to the boil, reduce the heat and simmer for 5 minutes. Remove from the heat and leave the beans to soak, still covered, for 2–4 hours. Then drain, rinse and cook in fresh water as above.

Whichever way you soak the beans, you may also cook them in their soaking water, adding if necessary extra water to make sure the beans are covered. This method preserves any vitamins that would otherwise be lost to the soaking water.

BELL PEPPERS
Green and red varieties are most often used and are almost always grilled and peeled before use. Throughout the text we have used the term 'bell peppers' rather than 'peppers' to distinguish them from chilli peppers.

To Skin Peppers
Grill or scorch them briefly over or under a flame, turning, until the skin begins to blister. Put, still hot, into a plastic bag and tie the end. Leave to steam for 10–15 minutes. Remove from the bag and peel the skin off under a running tap with your fingers or by using just kitchen paper and finger pressure. Note that skinned peppers do have a subtly different flavour to the unskinned variety and that they maintain the brightness of their colour.

To Roast Peppers
Preheat the oven to 450°F (230°C, gas mark 8). Rub the whole peppers with vegetable oil and place in a roasting tin. Place in the oven and roast for 40–45 minutes or until the peppers are soft and the skin obviously loose. Remove, allow to cool sufficiently to touch and then gently peel off the skin. Remove the seeds and discard, and then use or store the peppers in the refrigerator, just covered with oil. They will keep for up to 7 days.

CHILLI PEPPERS
Chilli peppers, members of the capsicum family, are indigenous to South and Central America. They grow in many shapes, sizes and

colours, with a hotness range that can produce anything from a warm glow in the mouth to the sensation of eating fire.

According to the cognoscenti of South American cuisine, each type of chilli has its own distinguishable flavour and a particular variety or combination of chillies may be necessary to give a specific dish its distinctive taste. For those of us unused to the subtle differences in flavour between chilli types (excluding their hotness which is of course easily recognized) and anyway probably unable to obtain a wide range, this finer aspect of Latin American cuisine is something we can only look forward to learning about. The recipes chosen for this book do not depend upon the availability of a specific type of chilli and you should feel free to substitute different chillies, as available, in the recipes.

Fresh unripe chillies are green, but as they ripen the colour may change to red, orange or yellow. If you are cutting fresh chillies, it is best to handle them wearing rubber gloves as they can irritate the skin. Do not touch your eyes with the gloves on. Wash the gloves immediately the job is finished. To reduce the fierceness of chilli peppers, remove the seeds and veins before chopping and adding them to a dish. Alternatively, leave them to soak in cold water for an hour before using. You can also add them whole and remove them before serving.

Dried chillies are as hot as the fresh variety, but because they contain no volatile oils they do not burn the skin as quickly. Red and green chillies are equally hot, though there is no method of predicting the strength of a particular chilli and even within the same batch some are hotter than others.

One teaspoon of hot pepper sauce used as a substitute for fresh or dried chillies is equivalent to 2 medium fresh or dried chilli peppers.

For reference, the main chilli types used in Latin American cooking are fresh serrano, jalapeño and poblano and dried ancho, guajillo, mulato, pasilla and chipotle. Canned pickled jalapeño chillies are also popular (these are now available in Europe in specialist shops).

Fresh chillies available in Britain include the following:

Jalapeño Normally the medium hot variety, they are imported from Kenya.

Serrano These are narrower and shorter than the jalapeño and usually hotter.

Habanero Range in colour from red to orange to yellow-green and in hotness from hot to extremely hot. They are commonly sold in West Indian and Asian grocery shops and are sometimes known as Scots bonnet.

European These long chillies with a pointed end are imported from Holland. They range from mild to fairly hot.

COCONUT MILK

Coconut milk is used quite extensively in Latin American cooking, as both a flavouring and a thickening agent. Coconut milk is not the liquid inside a coconut, which is called coconut water; it is the liquid pressed from grated coconut flesh diluted with water. In the West, it can be made from desiccated coconut or alternatively it can be bought canned in Chinese or Indian grocery stores. Use the unsweetened variety. There are two grades of coconut milk used in cooking – thick and thin. The category depends on whether the milk has been obtained from unpressed (thick) or once-pressed (thin) grated coconut flesh.

To Prepare Coconut Milk from Fresh Coconut
Makes 8 fl oz (225 ml) thick milk and 1 pint (550 ml) thin milk

Pierce the 'eyes' of a fresh coconut and drain off and reserve the coconut water. Place the whole coconut in a hot oven for about 10 minutes. Remove it from the oven, crack the outer shell and remove the pieces of coconut flesh. Peel off the brown outer skin with a vegetable peeler. Grate the flesh finely using a hand grater or blend it with 2 tablespoons (30 ml) of the coconut water. Place the grated or blended flesh in a saucepan and add 6 fl oz (175 ml) warm water. Gently heat but do not boil. Remove from the heat and allow to stand for 10 minutes. Press the contents of the pan through a fine sieve or piece of muslin cloth and collect the extraction, which is the *thick* milk. Heat to the boil 16 fl oz (450 ml) of water with the remaining coconut water, pour this over the coconut residue in the sieve and collect the extract. Press the flesh hard with the back of a spoon to get out all the liquid. The collected liquid is the *thin* milk.

Note: The recipes in this book use medium-thick milk. To make it follow the procedure above but use 12 fl oz (350 ml) warm water. The first extraction will then be of the right thickness. Alternatively, use canned coconut milk.

To Prepare Coconut Milk from Desiccated Coconut
Makes 1 pint (550 ml) medium-thick milk

Put 8 oz (225 g) desiccated coconut in a bowl and cover with 1 pint (550 ml) warm water. If you have a blender, put the mixture in, blend for 20 seconds and then filter the contents through á muslin cloth or fine sieve, collecting the liquid. Press the resultant mush hard to remove the last residue of juice. This produces the medium-thick coconut milk which is required for the recipes in this book.

If you do not have a blender, leave the coconut soaking in the water for 20 minutes and then squeeze and knead the mixture until it turns milky, and then filter. To make thin milk, repeat the above procedure, using the coconut mush in the sieve in place of the desiccated coconut. For very thick coconut milk (which is more appropriately called coconut cream) follow the above method but use half the volume of water.

Cooking with Coconut Milk

Coconut milk from either fresh grated or desiccated coconut should be used within 8 hours of being made. Canned coconut milk will keep in the fridge for 1–2 days after opening. Once coconut milk has been added to a dish, it should not be heated to more than a very gentle boil and the cooking pan or casserole dish containing the milk should not be covered. After adding the coconut milk, stir the dish continuously up to boiling point, then for at least 7 or 8 minutes afterwards. This ensures that the sauce is smooth and also prevents the milk from curdling or separating. Dishes cooked with coconut milk, if kept overnight, should be stored in the fridge.

MAIZE

The name maize probably derives from the name *mahis* given to the plant in the language of the native Indians of the Dominican Republic.

Maize, the only major cereal crop of American origin, is easy to grow and harvest and was eaten for thousands of years as a staple by the Aztec, Maya and Inca civilizations. The Spanish Conquistadores brought maize to Europe in the fifteenth century and the Portuguese then took it to Asia. It thrived and was a popular crop in both continents. However, in areas of the world where maize became the only staple food in an otherwise poor diet, it was later discovered that pellagra, a nutrient deficiency disease caused by lack of nicotinic acid, became prevalent. This had not been the case in the ancient civilizations of South America, because of the way they treated the maize kernels. They used a process, still in use today, in which the hulled, fresh or dried kernels are soaked and boiled in water to which charcoal (wood ash) or lime has been added. The swollen kernels are then drained and rinsed and the outer skins rubbed off. They may now be used immediately as a starch food like porridge (a dish called hominy in the USA) or pressed into a dough (*masa*) to make tortillas, or this dough is dried and ground into a flour (*masa harina*), later used to make tortilla dough. Treating the maize with alkali, present in the charcoal and lime, releases nicotinic acid, which is in fact present in the grain but which is bound up in the chemical niacytin. How the ancient Indians discovered this process is anyone's guess. In an ordinary mixed diet pellagra is not a problem associated with maize and the ease with which maize is cultivated has led to the development of many varieties, different in size, colour and flavour. Harold McGee in his book *On Food and Cooking* categorizes five main varieties of maize or corn (a generic term in most of the world, which can refer to a number of different grains but which in the Americas refers solely to maize):

> There are five different kinds of corn, each characterized by a different endosperm composition. Pop and flint corn have a relatively high protein content and hard rather than waxy starch. Dent corn, the variety most commonly grown for animal feed, has a localized deposit of soft, waxy starch at the crown of the kernal, which produces a depression, or dent, in the dried kernal. Flour corn, with little protein and mostly waxy starch, is grown only by native Americans for their own use. What we call Indian corn today are flour and flint varieties with variegated kernals. Finally, sweet corn, very popular as a vegetable when immature, stores more sugar than starch, and therefore has translucent kernals and loose, wrinkled skins (starch grains refract light and plump out the kernals in the other types). It appears that popcorn was the first kind of corn to be cultivated, but all five were known to native Americans long before the advent of Europeans.

The Andes mountains are home to the greatest variety of corns or maize. The Inca Indians developed the crop, but its botanical origins will possibly never be discovered. However, the Indians of Ecuador tell a story about its beginnings which is much more colourful than the real one is likely to be.

Many thousands of years ago there was a terrible flood and only two brothers survived. They did so by climbing to the top of the highest mountain in the land. Just as they were about to die of hunger and thirst, two gaily coloured parrots flew to them with food and drink, both made from the maize plant. The brothers were revitalized and one of them quickly captured one of the parrots. It turned into a beautiful woman, who gave them maize seeds and taught them how to plant and grow the crop. She became the mother of the first Indian tribe and maize became their basic food.

Maize and Nutrition

Whole maize products contain substantial amounts of phosphorus and iron and thiamine (Vitamin B_1) and smaller quantities of riboflavin (Vitamin B_2) and carotene, the precursor to Vitamin A. Whole maize has an average of 9 per cent by weight of protein. Eaten with other foods, particularly beans and vegetables, whole maize products are an excellent addition to the diet.

Maize Flour Products

To prepare whole maize, the grains are dried on the cob and then removed. However, maize is rarely eaten in this form, since milling it into flour increases its digestibility and the variety of ways it may be used. The fresh, tinned or frozen whole corn or maize kernels that we are familiar with are in fact obtained from sweetcorn, not flour corns. Sweetcorn or corn on the cob is too soft and too sweet to be dried and ground into a flour. It has a protein content that is slightly higher than many other vegetables, but lower than that of flour corns; its nutritional worth should really be compared with that of other fresh vegetables rather than other grains. The following descriptions refer to products made from flour corns, not sweetcorn.

Masa harina The whole grain is treated with an alkaline solution, dried and ground into a flour called *masa harina*. This is the flour traditionally used to make tortillas (see page 85). Ordinary corn-meal may be used to make tortillas, but the texture and flavour is different from those made with *masa harina*.

Whole maize flour or cornmeal The whole grain is ground into flour of 95 per cent to 100 per cent extraction. This flour or meal retains all the goodness of the maize. Stoneground is best if you can obtain it.

Bolted maize or cornmeal The whole grain is milled and then the coarse bran pieces are sifted out. This is 90 per cent to 95 per cent extraction meal or flour and it contains most of the goodness of the grain. It is better than whole maize for preparing breads or other dishes where a smooth mixture is desired.

Cornflour or Cornstarch (Degerminated Maize Meal) This is made from the whole grain with the bran and germ parts removed to give a flour of 85 per cent or less extraction. It is not as nutritious as whole maize flour, but is excellent for thickening soups and sauces. It is never used in the making of tortillas, tacos (see page 88) or other cornbreads.

Tortillas For an introduction to tortillas and associated products, see the chapter Tortillas, Tortilla Dishes and Breads (see page 85).

PLANTAINS

Plantains are a variety of banana that need to be cooked before eating. They are characterized by hard green skins and a dryish, starchy, fibrous flesh. Ripening plantains turn from green, through yellow to black, becoming sweeter all the time. Choose plantains that are large (8–12 in/20.5–30.5 cm) and firm, with green peel that may be flecked with some brown spots (although even with black peel they are still good, unless soft). They may be cooked in their skins whole, or topped and tailed, or peeled. Ripe ones are easily peeled, but green ones need to be cut along the ridges and the skin pared off with a knife. Peel under water to prevent staining of the hands. For roasting or barbecuing, slit the plantain skin from end to end and turn frequently during cooking. It will be tender in 15–20 minutes. Boiling green fruit in their skins takes about 30 minutes. For crisps, cut wafer-thin slices of green or half-ripe plantain and soak in cold water for 30 minutes before drying and frying.

TOMATOES

Tomatoes are used in many South American recipes. Vine-ripened tomatoes are the best to use rather than those picked green and ripened on the way to the supermarket shelves, but usually the latter are all we have available. Tinned, seeded tomatoes make a good substitute if fresh are unavailable. Most of the recipes in this book call for tomatoes to be skinned and seeded and instructions for doing this are given below. However, if you are in a hurry, this is not an absolute necessity. Small pieces of skin and the odd seed will be noticeable in the dish, but this is not a lot to worry about. Again, as an alternative, you may use tinned tomatoes.

Mexican cooks, especially, make use of green tomatoes, but these are not to be confused with unripe ordinary tomatoes. They are tomatoes in a green husk sometimes called tomatillos (*Physalis edulis*). They are used for their tart flavour and colour and are sometimes available in Europe in tins. Gooseberries make an excellent substitute.

To Skin and Seed Tomatoes

Plunge the raw tomatoes into a pot of boiling water. Count to fifteen, remove them with a slotted spoon and put into a pot or basin of cold water. The skin should now slip off rather easily. To remove the seeds, cut out the core, cut the tomatoes in half and squeeze out the seeds into a sieve. To get all the juice, press the seeds and collect the extract.

OTHER INGREDIENTS AND ALTERNATIVES

Cheese Mild and mature Cheddar, Parmesan and crumbly white Cheshire or Lancashire cheeses are the varieties most similar to those used in Latin American cooking.

Chayote This is a variety of squash (see page 54).

Herbs and Spices Coriander, bay, oregano, thyme, parsley and epazote (not easily available in the West) are the most commonly used herbs, and cinnamon, cloves, cumin, black peppercorns, paprika, vanilla pod and saffron are the most commonly used spices.

Limes These are used extensively as a seasoning.

Nuts Pine nuts, almonds, hazelnuts, raw unsalted peanuts and walnuts are widely used.

Olives Green are much more commonly used than black.

Quinoa Called 'the grain that grows where grass will not', quinoa is in fact the seed of an extremely hardy annual plant that grows in the Andes mountains. It contains good amounts of nutrients including protein and is easy to prepare. Quinoa was a staple food crop of the Inca Empire. It is now becoming available in Western grocery shops and supermarkets and is often used in the manufacture of meat-free convenience foods. Try it in salads (see page 51), for stuffing vegetables or in place of rice or other grains.

Rice Use long grain white rice (not pre or parcooked).

Sweet Potatoes Native to South America, the West Indies and the Pacific, they are now widely available in Asian and West Indian shops, markets and many supermarkets. The skin is generally pink, the shape long and knobbly, and the flesh either white, yellow or orange. They can be cooked in the same way as potatoes.

Appetizers and Snacks

Starters or hors d'œuvre are not a traditional part of a Latin American meal, although nowadays Western-style canapés are popular in more sophisticated circles. Appetizers and snack foods served with drinks and eaten between meals are, however, an intrinsic part of social life. Here we give recipes such as Avocado Filled with Raw Tomato Sauce, Aubergine Caviar and Toasted Chickpeas, while others, such as Tacos, Empanadas and Quesadillas and cornbreads, salads and dips like Guacamole, are given in other parts of the book.

Cheese on Toast (*Crostini*)   BRAZIL

Serves 4

This is an Italian-style snack. Sliced bread is spread with a chilli-hot cheese and butter mixture and grilled. Serve hot as a snack or appetizer with drinks.

8 medium-thick slices
wholemeal or white bread,
crusts removed if you wish
and quartered
2 oz (50 g) butter, softened
2 oz (50 g) Parmesan cheese,
finely grated

2 oz (50 g) Cheddar or
Gruyère cheese, finely
grated
½ teaspoon chilli sauce
black pepper to taste

Lightly toast the bread on one side. Combine the butter, cheese and chilli sauce and mix well together. Spread the mixture on the slices of bread, on the untoasted side, and season each with black pepper. Toast under the grill until the cheese colours brown. Serve hot.

Variation A cashew nut and cheese mixture may be substituted for the spread used above. To make, combine 2 oz (50 g) finely grated Parmesan cheese, 2 oz (50 g) finely grated Cheddar or Gruyère cheese, 2 tablespoons (30 ml) finely diced onion and ¼ teaspoon cayenne pepper. Spread this on the bread and grill as above. Meanwhile quickly dry roast 2 oz (50 g) unsalted chopped cashew nuts in a dry frying pan until lightly browned. Serve topped with the cashew nuts.

Chickpea Spread (*Colima de Garbanzos*)

Serves 4

This is a chilli-hot spread. For a milder version, reduce the number of chillies included. Use as a dip with tostadas (corn chips), crackers or crudités.

1 × 14 oz (400 g) can of
cooked chickpeas, drained
2 tablespoons (30 ml) olive oil
3 tablespoons (45 ml) lemon
juice

2 oz (50 g) cream cheese
3–6 small green chilli peppers,
seeded and cut into tiny dice
2 tablespoons (30 ml) roasted
pine nuts, roughly chopped

Put the chickpeas in a mixing bowl. Stir in all the other ingredients except the pine nuts. Process to a smooth paste in small amounts in a blender or food processor. Garnish with the chopped pine nuts and serve.

Toasted Chickpeas (*Garbanzo Compuesto*)

MEXICO

Makes 1 lb (450 g)

Serve these on their own or as an appetizer with drinks.

5 tablespoons (75 ml) olive oil
1 lb (450 g) cooked chickpeas
(use tinned chickpeas or
soak 6 oz (175 g) dried
chickpeas overnight, drain,
cover with fresh water and
cook until tender – see page
12)

2 cloves garlic, peeled and
finely chopped
salt and cayenne pepper to
taste

Heat the olive oil in a large frying pan. Make sure the cooked chickpeas are well drained of any liquid and then sauté them with the garlic in the hot olive oil. Stir and cook them until browned all over. Drain through a sieve and then spread on a piece of absorbent kitchen paper to soak up any excess oil. Sprinkle with salt and cayenne and serve.

Variation Peanuts, unsalted and skinned, may be treated in the same way as the chickpeas.

Baked Corn Torte (*Torta de Elote*)

ECUADOR

Serves 4

Serve as a light meal or as a rather rich first course. It is also good served with a Red Chilli and Paprika Tomato Sauce (see page 78)

kernels from 3 tender
sweetcorn cobs or 12 oz
(350 g) frozen sweetcorn
2 oz (50 g) butter
3 eggs

4 oz (100 g) Cheddar or
Cheshire cheese, grated
¼ pint (150 ml) milk
salt and white pepper to taste

Preheat the oven to 350°F (180°C, gas mark 4). Combine the corn, butter, eggs, cheese and milk in a blender or food processor and blend until the mixture is smooth. Season to taste with salt and white pepper. Spoon into a greased 2½ pint (1.5 litre soufflé dish or ring mould and bake in the preheated oven for 1 hour or until a knife or skewer inserted in the torte comes out clean. Turn out and serve hot or cold. The sauce suggested may also be served hot or cold.

Variation To make a potato or carrot or other vegetable torte, replace the corn kernels with 1 lb (450 g) cooked potato or carrot or other vegetable.

Aubergines Stuffed with Cheese   CHILE
(*Berenjena Rellena con Queso*)

Serves 4

Serve hot as part of a main course or as a cold appetizer. For a substantial dish, serve with a Basic Tomato sauce (see pages 79–80).

2 medium aubergines (about 2 lb/900 g)
salt
4 tablespoons (60 ml) olive oil
1 medium onion, peeled and finely chopped
4 oz (100 g) breadcrumbs
8 oz (225 g) Cheddar cheese, grated

salt and black pepper to taste
pinch of cayenne pepper
1 egg, lightly beaten
4 tablespoons (60 ml) finely grated Parmesan cheese
1 oz (25 g) butter

Cut the aubergines in half lengthwise, score the flesh surfaces with a sharp knife and sprinkle salt over them. Set aside for 30 minutes, then rinse under a cold tap and pat dry with absorbent kitchen paper. With a sharp pointed knife cut the flesh out of each half aubergine leaving a ½ in (1.2 cm) shell. Coarsely chop the flesh.

Preheat the oven to 375°F (190°C, gas mark 5). Heat the olive oil in a frying pan and sauté the onion until softened and golden. Stir in the aubergine flesh and cook, stirring, for 2–3 minutes. Remove from the heat and stir in the breadcrumbs, cheese, salt and black pepper to taste, cayenne and beaten egg. Fill the aubergine shells with this mixture and place them on a greased baking tray or dish. Sprinkle Parmesan cheese over each, dot with butter and return to the preheated oven for 30 minutes.

Peppers Stuffed with Corn and Cream Cheese (*Pimientos Rellenos con Maiz y Queso Crema*)

Serves 4

These make a colourful starter, particularly with the topping of tomato sauce. They are easy but quite time-consuming to prepare, though they can be put together in advance and then baked when needed.

4 large green bell peppers
1 tablespoon (15 ml) vegetable oil
1 medium onion, peeled and finely chopped
2 cloves garlic, peeled and finely chopped
8 oz (225 g) fresh or frozen sweetcorn

1 fresh red or green chilli pepper, seeded and finely chopped
salt to taste
4 oz (100 g) cream cheese
4 tablespoons (60 ml) pomegranate seeds (optional)
1 recipe quantity Basic Tomato Sauce (see page 79)

Grill and skin the peppers (see page 13). Cut down one side of each pepper and carefully extract the seeds, leaving the veins in place. Set aside. Heat the oil in a pan, add the onion and garlic and stir and cook until softened. Add the corn kernels and chilli, stir, reduce the heat, cover and cook until the corn is tender. Remove from the heat, season to taste with salt and stir in the cream cheese and pomegranate seeds, if using. Set aside to cool. Preheat the oven to 350°F (180°C, gas mark 4). Carefully fill the peppers with the mixture and place them in a lightly greased baking dish. If the open seams do not overlap easily you can close them with a toothpick pushed into one side and then the other. Cover with the tomato sauce and bake in the preheated oven for 20 minutes. Serve hot.

Avocado Filled with Raw Tomato Sauce
(*Paltas Rellenas con Salsa Cruda*)   BOLIVIA

Serves 4–6

2 medium tomatoes, skinned
  (see page 19) and chopped
1 medium onion, peeled and
  finely chopped
¼ green bell pepper, seeded
  and finely chopped

salt and black pepper to taste
1 teaspoon wine vinegar
1 tablespoon (15 ml) olive oil
3 ripe avocados

Make the sauce by combining all the ingredients except the avocados and mixing well together. Halve the avocados, remove the stones and fill them with prepared sauce. Serve immediately.

Stuffed Apples (*Macas Recheadas*)   BRAZIL

Serves 4

This dish of apples stuffed with vegetables in a cream sauce may be served as a cold starter or as a side dish. You could experiment with fillings. We have suggested a mixture of cooked vegetables, but grains and/or beans could be added to the mix.

4 eating apples
juice of 1 lemon
8 fl oz (225 ml) single cream
1 teaspoon prepared mustard
  (mild or strong)

8 oz (225 g) mixed lightly
  cooked cold vegetables, such
  as carrots, peas and onions
salt and black pepper to taste

Cut the tops off the apples leaving a flat surface. Cut out the flesh from each leaving a shell about ¾ in (2 cm) in thickness. Brush the exposed surfaces with lemon juice. Combine the cream, mustard, vegetables (leave aside 1 tablespoon (15 ml)) and remaining lemon juice and season with salt and black pepper. Stuff the apple shells with the mixture and serve each garnished with a portion of the reserved cooked vegetables.

Aubergine Caviar (*Caviar de Berenjena*)

Serves 4

Serve as a starter with corn tortilla chips or as a side salad.

2 lb (900 g) aubergines
4 tablespoons (60 ml) olive oil
1 tablespoon (15 ml) lime or
  lemon juice
1 green or red bell pepper,
  skinned (see page 13),
  seeded and finely chopped

1 medium onion, peeled and
  finely chopped
2 medium tomatoes, finely
  chopped
2 tablespoons (30 ml) finely
  chopped fresh coriander
salt and black pepper to taste

Preheat the oven to 375°F (190°C, gas mark 5) and bake the aubergines until tender (30–45 minutes depending on the size). Remove from the oven and set aside to cool. Meanwhile combine the olive oil and lime or lemon juice. Combine the remaining ingredients. Peel the aubergine and chop the flesh into largish chunks. Mix together the onion, bell pepper and tomato mixture, the oil and lemon or lime juice dressing and the aubergine and serve on a bed of lettuce.

Tomato and Cheese Salad

Serves 4

Serve as a starter, side salad or for a light lunch.

1–2 fresh red or green chilli
  peppers, seeded
3 large tomatoes, skinned,
  seeded (see page 19) and
  chopped
6 oz (175 g) hard cheese,
  cubed

2–3 spring onions, finely
  chopped
2 tablespoons (30 ml) finely
  chopped coriander
1 tablespoon (15 ml) olive oil
2 teaspoons lime juice
salt to taste

Cover the chillies in boiling water, leave for 5 minutes, drain and finely chop. Stir all the ingredients together, chill and serve.

Variation For a simple tomato salad, leave out the cheese.

Caribbean Salad (*Ensalada del Caribe*)   BELIZE

Serves 4

This salad can be made all the year round, but it is cooling and refreshingly sweet on a hot summer's day. It is also good as an exotic and colourful starter for a winter meal that needs cheering up.

4 in (10 cm) piece of cucumber, quartered lengthwise and chopped crosswise

2 medium just-ripe bananas, peeled and thinly sliced

2 medium green bell peppers, seeded, cored and diced

2 sweet oranges, peeled, pith removed and separated into segments, which are cut in half

5 fl oz (150 ml) natural yoghurt

1 tablespoon (15 ml) flaked almonds, lightly toasted

Combine the cucumber, bananas, green peppers and oranges in a salad bowl. Stir in the yoghurt, sprinkle almonds over the top, chill and serve.

Potato and Parsley Salad (*Ensalada de Papas y Perejil*)

Serves 4

Serve this simple but tasty salad as a side dish or on its own before the main course.

1 lb (450 g) small potatoes, scrubbed or peeled and chopped

4 tablespoons (60 ml) olive oil

1 tablespoon (15 ml) wine vinegar

salt and black pepper to taste

3 tablespoons (45 ml) finely chopped parsley

Cook the potatoes until only just tender. Drain and while still hot pour over the oil, then the vinegar and season with salt and black pepper. Mix gently. Add parsley and mix again. Serve warm or cold.

Ranch-Style Eggs (*Huevos Rancheros*)   MEXICO

Serves 2–4

This makes a filling breakfast for a cold morning. If tortillas are not available, substitute thick slices of wholemeal bread.

vegetable oil for frying
1 medium onion, peeled and
   finely chopped
1 clove garlic, peeled and
   finely chopped
1–2 fresh or dried red or green
   chilli peppers, seeded and
   finely chopped

8 oz (225 g) tinned tomatoes,
   drained and chopped
4 tortillas (see pages 85–88)
4 eggs
cheese and/or avocado slices,
   to garnish (optional)

Heat 2 tablespoons (30 ml) oil in a frying pan and sauté the onion, garlic and chillies until the onion is softened. Add the tomatoes, stir and gently cook for 5 minutes. Meanwhile, in another frying pan, fry the tortillas quickly on both sides in a little oil and set on warmed serving plates. In the same pan add oil and fry the eggs. Arrange the eggs on the tortillas, pour over the sauce, garnish and serve immediately.

Soups

Soup is very popular throughout Latin America and no proper meal would begin without a bowl of piping hot soup, summer or winter. In poorer regions, where people have to live off the land and even then have a struggle to make anything grow, soup is often the mainstay of a meal.

Sopas can range from light to substantial and from liquid to dry. In Mexico, for example, *sopa de arroz* has all its liquid steamed off and the finished dish is similar to fried rice or risotto, while Peruvian *chupes* or chowders are thick milky broths, solid with many combinations of vegetables. Soup of itself is not indigenous to South American cooking. It was introduced by the Spanish colonists, but the indigenous Indian method of slow cooking, where the savoury goodness of ingredients was maximized by long simmering, lent itself perfectly to the making of wonderful soups. New ingredients were combined with local produce. In particular, squashes and beans of every shape, size and colour were transformed into soups.

Purées of soup have also become popular, although not enriched or thickened with cream in the European manner. In Brazil, they use pumpkin as a thickening agent, but in other cuisines flours and meals are employed, especially rice, tapioca, potatoes and potato flour. Cheese is also sometimes used, both as a thickening and to add flavour to soups.

Cold soups generally are not popular, although *gazpacho* is enjoyed in Mexico and *sopa de palta*, an avocado soup which is usually served chilled, is widely made.

The best Latin American soup, simple or elaborate, delicate or hearty, must have a good flavour, an appetizing colour and, naturally, a flash of fire!

Vegetable Stock (*Caldo de Verduras*)

Makes 3 pints (1.7 litres)

It is important to remember that to make a really well-flavoured soup, it is best to use stock. However, if you have not got the time to make any, the water saved from cooking vegetables will help the soup a great deal. So also will the liquor left from cooking pulses. If you have nothing like these to hand and you are in a hurry, vegetable stock cubes dissolved in water are generally adequate and even yeast extract (using 1 teaspoon to ¾–1 pint (450–550 ml) of boiling water) imparts a reasonably good flavour. However, making a proper vegetable stock is a simple business and worth doing if you have the time. Root vegetables tend to make the best stocks, while green vegetables such as Brussels sprouts and cabbage should be avoided (they make the flavour too strong and even bitter). The recipe given here does not include salt, since you may wish to use the stock to make, say, a bean soup which is best salted at the end of cooking.

4 large potatoes	8 cloves garlic, bruised
2 carrots	2 tablespoons (30 ml) olive oil
1 large onion, peeled and chopped	2½ pints (1.5 litres) water
	1 bay leaf
2 sticks of celery	1 sprig of fresh thyme

Scrub all the vegetables, but do not peel them. Chop them all roughly. Fry the vegetables gently in the olive oil in a large saucepan. If a pale stock is wanted, do not let them colour. If a darker stock is required, fry them until they begin to brown. Now add the water and the herbs, bring to the boil, then cover and allow to simmer for 1½–2 hours. Strain and reserve the liquid. It will keep for 3–4 days in a refrigerator and can also be frozen.

Avocado Soup (*Sopa de Palta*)

Serves 4

This beautiful pale green soup can be made in minutes. Its velvety texture and buttery richness make it popular from Mexico to Chile.

2 large ripe avocados
juice of ½ a lemon or 1 lime
1 pint (550 ml) cooled
  vegetable stock
½ pint (275 ml) single cream
salt and ground white pepper
  to taste

1 tablespoon (15 ml) finely
  chopped fresh coriander
  leaves
4 tortillas (see pages 85–8),
  quartered and fried crisp in
  corn oil

Halve the avocados, remove the stones, scoop out the flesh, place it in a bowl with the lemon or lime juice and mash with a fork. Add the vegetable stock and the cream and stir well. Beat lightly with a wire whisk to make the soup a little smoother. Season to taste with salt and pepper. Stir in the coriander, reserving some for garnish. Chill and serve with the fried tortillas.

If you wish to serve this soup warm, put the mashed avocados in a warmed tureen and pour on the stock, which has been heated through with the cream. Whisk and serve as before.

Broad Bean Soup (*Caldo de Habas Secas*)   MEXICO

Serves 6

The broad bean was grown in South America at least 5,000 years ago. It has travelled the earth.

1 small onion, peeled and
  chopped
2 cloves garlic, peeled and
  chopped
1 tablespoon (15 ml) olive oil
8 oz (225 g) dried broad
  beans, soaked overnight in
  cold water
12 oz (350 g) tomatoes,
  skinned (see page 19) and
  chopped

2½ pints (1.5 litres) water
2 sprigs of fresh mint
1 oz (25 g) fresh coriander
  leaves, chopped roughly,
  plus a few whole leaves to
  garnish
several dashes of Tabasco
  sauce
salt and black pepper to taste
2 oz (50 g) feta cheese,
  crumbled

Fry the onion and garlic in a large saucepan in the olive oil until softened. Add the beans and tomatoes and cook until reduced a little. Add the water and herbs and simmer for 1½–2 hours, or until the beans are tender. Add the Tabasco and season with salt and pepper. Serve in large bowls, garnished with crumbled feta and coriander leaves.

Coconut Soup
(*Sopa de Crema de Coco*)

COLOMBIA

Serves 4–6

This unusual and exotic soup is from Colombia, where coconut is used in many dishes.

1 oz (25 g) butter	¾ pint (450 ml) milk
1 medium onion, peeled and finely chopped	7 oz (200 g) block creamed coconut, roughly chopped
¼ teaspoon grated nutmeg	1 pint (550 ml) vegetable stock
2 tablespoons (30 ml) cornflour	salt to taste
	¼ pint (150 ml) single cream

Melt the butter in a large saucepan. Fry the onion in it until soft and translucent. Add the nutmeg. Blend the cornflour with a little of the milk to make a smooth paste and set aside. Add the remaining milk, the creamed coconut, the stock and a little salt to the onions in the saucepan and heat through, stirring. When almost boiling, add the blended cornflour and stir until smooth and thickened. Add the cream and reheat but do not boil. Serve in bowls with a dash of nutmeg on top.

Cold Soup (*Gazpacho*)

Serves 4–6

Gazpacho is a true peasant soup which has been modified and made increasingly sophisticated, so that today the vegetables predominate more than the robust bread porridge, flavoured with olive oil, vinegar and garlic, of old. Here is a Mexican version of this old Spanish dish.

1½ slices of day-old bread
½ pint (275 ml) water
1 tablespoon (15 ml) white
   wine vinegar
1 clove garlic, peeled and
   crushed
1 large cucumber, peeled,
   seeded and diced
1 lb (450 g) ripe tomatoes,
   skinned (see page 19) and
   roughly chopped

1 avocado, peeled, halved,
   stoned and diced
1 green bell pepper, seeded
   and diced
1 tablespoon (15 ml) olive oil
¼ pint (150 ml) canned tomato
   juice
salt to taste

Put the bread to soak in a few tablespoons of the water with the vinegar and the garlic for 15 minutes. Mix the cucumber, tomatoes, avocado and green pepper together in a bowl and set aside. Either purée the soaked bread and garlic in a blender or pound in a mortar, then add the olive oil, tomato juice and the rest of the water and blend until smooth. Pour into a soup tureen or large serving bowl and stir in the diced vegetables. Season with salt. Put in the refrigerator for at least 1 hour. Serve the soup as chilled as possible.

Cabbage and Potato Soup
(*Caldo Verde*)

BRAZIL

Serves 4

This classic soup was brought to Brazil by the Portuguese who settled there. Drumhead cabbage is most suitable for this soup, but it must be finely shredded. The cabbage is only very lightly cooked.

3 medium potatoes, peeled
   and roughly chopped
1 pint (550 ml) water
pinch of salt
2 tablespoons (30 ml) olive oil

8 oz (225 g) cabbage, finely
   shredded
salt and black pepper to taste

Cook the potatoes until tender in the water with a pinch of salt. Drain, reserve the cooking liquor, and mash the potatoes. Return them to the cooking liquor, stir and add the olive oil and shredded cabbage. Boil for 3 minutes, uncovered. Season to taste with salt and pepper. Serve hot.

Garlic Soup (*Sopa de Ajo*) MEXICO

Serves 4

Garlic soup has an honoured and ancient place in Mexican cuisine. It is not strongly flavoured, but delicate, and few would guess correctly the main ingredient. This soup with its poached egg and cheese garnish makes a fine lunch or supper dish.

12 plump cloves garlic
pinch of salt
2 oz (50 g) butter
1 teaspoon plain flour
1½ pints (900 ml) vegetable stock
few drops of Tabasco sauce

salt and black pepper to taste
4 eggs
2 oz (50 g) feta cheese, crumbled
1 tablespoon (15 ml) finely chopped parsley

Mash the garlic on a chopping board as finely as possible with the flat of a knife blade and a little salt (in this way it becomes a purée quite quickly). Melt the butter in a large saucepan, add the garlic and the flour and fry gently for a few minutes. Stir in the vegetable stock and boil for 15 minutes. Strain and return to the heat. Season to taste with the Tabasco, salt and pepper. With the soup at a gentle simmer, slip in the eggs carefully, one at a time. When the eggs are poached, serve the soup, with an egg in each bowl and the feta cheese and parsley sprinkled over the top.

Green Pea Soup (*Sopa de Chícharos*) MEXICO

Serves 4–6

This soup, made from one of Mexico's favourite vegetables, brings out the full sweet flavour of the garden pea.

2 oz (50 g) finely chopped parsley
3 oz (75 g) butter
a good pinch of nutmeg
salt
1 egg
2 medium onions, peeled and thinly sliced

2 pints (1.2 litres) vegetable stock
1 lb (450 g) shelled fresh green peas
1 avocado, peeled, halved, stoned and thinly sliced

Mix the chopped parsley with 1 oz (25 g) butter, the nutmeg and a pinch of salt. Beat the egg lightly and then blend into the parsley mixture. Leave to stand on one side for 15 minutes. Meanwhile, fry the onions gently until soft in the remaining butter in a large saucepan. Add the vegetable stock and bring to the boil. Add the peas and simmer gently for 5 minutes, then gradually drop in the parsley mixture from a teaspoon while cooking until the peas are tender. Season to taste and serve in bowls, garnished with the sliced avocado.

Tomato and Corn Chowder (*Sopa de Elote Roja*)

Serves 6

This basic South American soup is quick to prepare, tasty and filling.

1 tablespoon (15 ml) olive oil	2½ pints (1.5 litres) vegetable
1 onion, peeled and chopped	stock
1 clove garlic, peeled and	1 lb (450 g) fresh or frozen
chopped	sweetcorn
1 lb (450 g) tomatoes,	salt and ground black pepper
skinned, seeded (see page	to taste
19) and chopped or 1 × 14	4 thin slices of mozzarella
oz (400 g) can of plum	cheese
tomatoes, roughly chopped	tabasco sauce to taste

Heat the olive oil in a large saucepan and soften the onion and garlic in it without browning. Add the tomatoes, cover and cook for 10 minutes. Add the stock and bring to the boil, then add the corn kernels and simmer for almost 10 minutes or until just tender. Season to taste. This soup can be served as it is, with plenty of texture, or blended to a smooth purée. Whichever you choose, reheat it gently and serve really hot with a slice of mozzarella and a dash of tabasco in each bowl.

Swiss Chard Chowder (*Guisado de Acelgas*)

Serves 4

A *guisado* is similar to a stew and this dish is a really filling meal in itself.

4 medium potatoes, peeled
    and cooked
1 small onion, peeled and
    finely chopped
2 cloves garlic, peeled and
    finely chopped
3 tablespoons (45 ml) olive oil
1 × 14 oz (400 g) can of plum
    tomatoes

1 × 14 oz (400 g) can of
    cooked chickpeas, drained
1 lb (450 g) Swiss chard,
    cooked in almost no water,
    drained and chopped
salt to taste

Quarter the potatoes and put in a deep platter or soup tureen. In a large saucepan, fry the onion and garlic lightly in the olive oil. Purée the tomatoes, pass through a sieve and add, together with the chickpeas and Swiss chard to the onions and garlic. Season with salt. Stir well and bring to the boil. Pour over the potatoes and serve immediately.

Variation If Swiss chard is not available, leaf spinach will substitute very well.

Cream of Celeriac Soup (*Crema de Apio*)

VENEZUELA

Serves 4–6

Apio is Spanish for both celery and celeriac and this rich soup from Venezuela uses both vegetables.

12 oz (350 g) celeriac
juice of ½ lemon
4 oz (100 g) celery
2 tablespoons (30 ml) olive oil
1 large clove garlic, peeled and
    finely chopped
1 large onion, peeled and
    finely chopped
½ teaspoon fennel seeds
½ teaspoon ground turmeric
a pinch of cayenne pepper

1 medium leek, white part
    only, washed and finely
    chopped
8 fl oz (225 ml) dry white wine
1 teaspoon sugar
1 pint (550 ml) vegetable stock
salt to taste
2 tablespoons (30 ml) chopped
    fresh dill

Trim and peel the celeriac. Wash and divide into two. Grate or julienne one half. Put the grated celeriac into a bowl, cover with cold water and add the lemon juice. Mix well and set aside. Coarsely chop the remaining celeriac and set aside. Wash, trim and slice the celery. In a large saucepan, heat the olive oil. Add the garlic, onion, fennel seeds, turmeric and cayenne. Fry gently until the onion is soft and translucent. Add the leek, celery, wine and sugar. Turn up the heat and cook, stirring, until all the liquid has evaporated. Add the coarsely chopped celeriac and the vegetable stock. Stir well. Bring to the boil, lower the heat and simmer for 10–15 minutes. Remove from the heat, cool a little and purée in batches in a blender or food processor. It should be the consistency of double cream. If too thick add a little water. Pour the puréed soup into a double boiler. Drain off the julienned or grated celeriac and add to the soup, reserving 2 tablespoons (30 ml). Allow to heat through for about 10 minutes. Season to taste with salt. Sprinkle with chopped dill and garnish with the reserved celeriac strips. Serve at once.

Thick Bean and Vegetable Soup   BRAZIL
(*Ensopado com Feijao e Legumes*)

Serves 4–6

Serve this robust soup from Brazil with slices of dark rye bread and cucumber, sliced thinly and toss in soured cream.

6 oz (175 g) haricot beans, soaked overnight in cold water	8 fl oz (225 ml) water
	6 fl oz (175 ml) dry white wine
	1 lb (450 g) tomatoes, skinned
2 vegetable stock cubes	(see page 19) and chopped
2 oz (50 g) butter	1 bay leaf
8 oz (225 g) onions, peeled and chopped	1 teaspoon dried basil
	salt and black pepper to taste
8 oz (225 g) parsnips, peeled and chopped	grated rind of ½ lemon

Drain the beans. Just cover with fresh water, add the stock cubes and boil in a large casserole for 30–40 minutes, until cooked but not mushy. Set aside. Heat the butter in a saucepan, add the onions and fry until soft and golden. Add the parsnips and cook until soft. Add these vegetables to the beans in the casserole. Put the water and wine in the pan in which the onions and parsnips were cooked and bring to the boil. Simmer for 1 minute, then pour over the beans. Add the chopped tomatoes, bay leaf and basil to the beans. Mix everything together lightly with a wooden spoon. Cover with a lid and simmer over a low heat for 45 minutes. Serve in bowls, garnished with the grated lemon rind.

Pumpkin Soup (*Api Zapallo*) ARGENTINA

Serves 4

This golden yellow soup from Argentina may be served as a first course if a light main course follows, or as a complete meal with a salad and wholemeal bread.

2 oz (50 g) butter
2 medium onions, peeled and finely chopped
2–3 cloves garlic, peeled and finely chopped
2 large tomatoes, skinned, seeded (see page 19) and chopped
¼ teaspoon cayenne pepper

½ teaspoon ground cumin
2 lb (900 g) pumpkin, peeled, seeded and diced
1 pint (550 ml) water
¼ teaspoon sugar
4 oz (100 g) Cheddar cheese, grated
¼ pint (150 ml) milk
salt to taste

Melt the butter in a large saucepan. Add the onions, garlic, tomatoes and spices. Fry until the onion is softened but not too coloured. Add the pumpkin and stir well. Pour over the water. Bring to the boil, lower the heat, cover and simmer for 20 minutes, until the pumpkin has disintegrated. Add the sugar. Mash the pumpkin a little, but not too much so that it retains some texture. Stir in the cheese and milk. Season to taste with salt and serve hot.

Variation In Chile the soup is made thinner and 2 eggs are beaten and added to it at the last minute.

Pine Nut Soup (*Sopa de Piñones*)

Serves 4

The *piñon* or pine nut is an important source of food for the Pueblo Indians of New Mexico. These sweet, rich nuts make a delicious nutritious soup, but are expensive, so reserve for special days.

1 bunch of spring onions, chopped (white and green parts)
1 lb (450 g) pine nuts
12 coriander seeds, crushed

1 teaspoon dried mint
½ pint (275 ml) milk
1 pint (550 ml) vegetable stock
salt and black pepper to taste

Set aside half of the chopped spring onions. Combine all the remaining ingredients in a saucepan, bring to the boil, lower the heat and

simmer, stirring from time to time, for 30–40 minutes. Remove
from the heat, cool and purée in a blender or food processor. Reheat
gently and stir in the reserved spring onions. Serve hot.

Peanut Soup (*Sopa de Amendoim*)   BOLIVIA

Serves 4

Peanut soup is common throughout Latin America, though there
are many different versions. This one comes from Bolivia.

3 oz (75 g) roasted peanuts,
   ground fairly finely in a
   blender
3 oz (75 g) rice flour
1 egg
¼ pint (150 ml) milk or single
   cream

1½ pints (900 ml) vegetable
   stock
salt and ground black pepper
2 tablespoons (30 ml) chopped
   parsley or chives

Mix the ground peanuts and rice flour in a small bowl. Beat the egg
and milk or cream together lightly and stir into the peanuts and
flour. Bring the vegetable stock to the boil in a saucepan. Drizzle in
the peanut mixture. Cover the pan and simmer over a low heat for
15 minutes. Season to taste with salt and pepper. Add herbs of your
choice and serve.

Lentil Soup with Banana
(*Sopa de Lentejas con Plátano*)

Serves 4–6

Lentils and banana make an unlikely but delicious combination in
this filling soup.

8 oz (225 g) brown lentils
2 pints (1.2 litres) water
1 small onion, peeled
1 clove garlic, peeled
12 oz (350 g) tomatoes (beef
   steak tomatoes are best)
salt and black pepper

1 tablespoon (15 ml) olive oil
1 large banana
2 tablespoons (30 ml) chopped
   parsley
tabasco sauce to taste

Cover the lentils with the water. Add the whole onion and garlic
clove and simmer for about 30–35 minutes, until the lentils are soft.

Meanwhile, grill the tomatoes until they are soft and the skins have blistered. Remove the onion and garlic from the lentil pot and purée them with the tomatoes in a blender. Season the purée with salt and pepper. In another saucepan, heat the oil until very hot. Put in the purée and cook over a medium heat, stirring all the time, until the sauce is thick and reduced a little. Pour the lentils and their liquid on to this sauce and cook for a further 20 minutes to mingle all the flavours. Peel and slice the banana thickly on the diagonal. Add to the soup and simmer for a further 5 minutes. Prior to serving, add the chopped parsley and a few dashes of tabasco sauce to taste.

Mint Soup (*Sopa de Hortela*) BRAZIL
Serves 4

This soup from Brazil, with a hint of the exotic, tastes delicious and looks wonderful with the poached eggs floating in a pale green 'sea'.

3 tablespoons (45 ml) olive oil
2 cloves garlic, peeled and
 crushed
2 pints (1.2 litres) vegetable
 stock
1 bunch of fresh mint (at least
 2 oz (50 g)), roughly

chopped, plus 4 sprigs to
 garnish
salt and black pepper to taste
4 eggs
4 slices of French bread,
 toasted

In a medium-sized saucepan, heat the olive oil. Add the garlic and cook, stirring, until it softens but is not browned. Add the stock and chopped mint and bring to the boil over a medium heat. Lower the heat and simmer for 10 minutes, then remove from the heat, cool and purée in a blender or food processor. Return to the cleaned pan and heat until simmering gently. Season to taste. Break the eggs into the simmering soup and allow them to poach for 2 minutes. Place a slice of French bread in the bottom of 4 heated soup bowls. Ladle in the soup over the bread, so that a poached egg is floating in each bowl. Garnish each bowl with a sprig of fresh mint and serve.

Salads

Salads in Latin America tend to be simple and as a rule often consist of just a selection of lightly cooked or raw vegetables, dressed separately in vinaigrette. Fortunately, however, there are exceptions and, since we particularly like salads, we have managed to search out and include here a number of the more unusual recipes, combining both familiar and exotic ingredients into colourful and tasty salad dishes.

Vegetable Salad   ECUADOR
(Ensalada de Verduras)

Serves 4–6

Ecuador is only 15 miles from the equator, so that all year round they have equal hours of day and night. Twelve hours of sunshine each day allows the cultivation of an abundant variety of fruits and vegetables, and Ecuadorian cuisine is well known for its imaginative use of these foods. This salad is in fact very simple, but it requires good quality ingredients. A selection of raw or lightly cooked vegetables is arranged in an attractive pattern on a platter, dressed with vinaigrette and served as a separate course before the main dish.

1 recipe quantity Basic
  Vinaigrette Dressing (see
  page 82)
1½ lb (750 g) vegetables,
  selected from the following:

Cooked (the vegetables should
  retain their colour and some
  crunch) artichoke hearts,
  quartered; asparagus, cut
  into 1 in (2.5 cm) lengths;

beetroot, diced; carrots,
  diced; cauliflower, in florets;
  sweetcorn; green beans, cut
  into 1 in (2.5 cm) lengths;
  green peas; okra; potatoes,
  diced

Raw avocados, sliced; celery,
  chopped; tomatoes, sliced

Prepare and dress the vegetables separately and then arrange on a serving platter.

Jerusalem Artichoke Salad
(*Ensalada de Alcachofas*)

CHILE

Serves 4

This makes a change from the more usual potato salad.

2 lb (900 g) large Jerusalem
  artichokes, washed and
  scraped
salt

1 recipe quantity Basic
  Vinaigrette Dressing (see
  page 82)

Cook the Jerusalem artichokes in a pan of boiling salted water until just tender but not soft and mushy. Drain, leave to cool, slice and then toss with the salad dressing. Serve.

Cauliflower Salad
(*Ensalada de Coliflor*)

MEXICO

Serves 4

The white of the cauliflower showing beneath the soft green sauce makes this an extremely attractive dish to look at.

1 medium cauliflower, divided
  into florets
salt

1 recipe quantity Guacamole
  (see page 83)

Cook the cauliflower florets in boiling salted water until only just tender (7–8 minutes). Drain, allow to cool, then pour over the guacamole and serve immediately. The guacamole will start to discolour if you leave it too long.

Whole Cauliflower Salad   DOMINICAN REPUBLIC
(*Ensalada de Colifor Entera*)

Serves 4

In this variation on the previous recipe, the cauliflower is cooked whole and then dressed in an avocado and almond sauce. This dish looks imposing as part of a buffet.

1 medium cauliflower	2 tablespoons (30 ml)
salt	vegetable oil
1 large ripe avocado	2 oz (50 g) ground almonds
1 tablespoon (15 ml) white	2 fl oz (50 ml) milk
wine vinegar or lemon juice	salt and black pepper to taste

Cook the cauliflower whole in a large pan of boiling salted water until only just tender (it should retain a slight crunch in the texture). Place in a serving dish and set aside to cool. Cut the avocado in half, remove the stone and scrape the flesh into a mixing bowl or blender. Add the remaining ingredients and beat or blend into a smooth consistency. Pour the sauce over the cauliflower (either still warm or cold) and serve immediately.

Corn Salad (*Salada de Milho*)   BRAZIL

Serves 4

3 sweetcorn cobs, cooked and the kernels scraped off, or 1 × 16 oz (450 g) can of sweetcorn, drained	½ medium onion, peeled and finely chopped
1 small red bell pepper, seeded and finely chopped	1 clove garlic, peeled and finely chopped
1 small green bell pepper, seeded and finely chopped	½ recipe quantity Basic Vinaigrette Dressing (see page 82)

Combine the corn kernels, peppers, onion, garlic and dressing. Cover, chill for 1 hour and serve.

Spinach, Apple and Lime Salad   ARGENTINA
(*Ensalada de Espinacas, Manzana y Lima*)

Serves 4

In this salad the sharpness of the lime juice sets off the sweetness of the apple and the flavour also enhances the sometimes harsh taste of spinach.

1 lb (450 g) fresh spinach,
    washed and drained
2 tablespoons (30 ml)
    vegetable oil
1 tablespoon (15 ml) lime
    juice

2 medium eating apples,
    chilled, cored, quartered and
    chopped into small pieces
salt and black pepper to taste

Remove any thick spinach stalks and finely shred the leaves. Combine the oil and lime juice and whisk well together. Mix the spinach and the chilled apples. Pour the oil and lime dressing over this mixture and add salt and black pepper. Toss well and serve.

Sweet Red Pepper Salad   URUGUAY
(*Ensalada de Pimientos Rojos Dulces*)

Serves 4

This salad has a rich flavour and it is best served in small amounts or with other lighter salads.

3–4 firm red bell peppers,
    skinned (see page 13) and
    seeded
8 large firm olives
1 clove garlic, peeled and
    crushed

2 tablespoons (30 ml) olive oil
1 tablespoon (15 ml) lemon or
    lime juice
salt and pepper to taste

Cut the peppers into ½ in (1.2 cm) wide strips and place in a small mixing bowl. Cut the olives in half and remove the stones. If the olives have tough skins it is a simple and worthwhile task to peel these off. Slice the olives into small crescents and add them and the remaining ingredients to the peppers. Mix gently but thoroughly, cover and leave in a cool place for at least 2 hours for the flavours to develop. Adjust the seasoning before serving.

Avocado and Pineapple Salad   HAITI
(*Ensalada de Aguacate y Piña*)

Serves 4

1 large ripe avocado, flesh
   removed and cut into small
   chunks
8 oz (225 g) fresh or tinned
   pineapple chunks
2 tablespoons (30 ml)
   vegetable oil

1 tablespoon (15 ml) lemon
   juice
salt and black pepper to taste
finely chopped parsley to
   garnish

Place the avocado and pineapple in a large bowl. Mix together the oil,
lemon juice and seasoning and pour over the avocado and pineapple.
Carefully mix together so as not to crush the avocado too much. Transfer to individual serving bowls or plates, garnish with parsley and serve.

Courgette, Green Bean, Apple and   MEXICO
Pomegranate Salad
(*Ensalada de Calabacitas, Ejotes Verdes,*
Manzana y Granada)

Serves 4

This unusual combination of ingredients works well and provides a
colourful substantial salad.

12 oz (350 g) courgettes, cut
   into 1 in (2.5 cm) rounds
12 oz (350 g) green beans, cut
   into 2 in (5 cm) lengths
2 medium apples, peeled,
   cored and chopped
4 fl oz (100 ml) vegetable oil

4 fl oz (100 ml) natural
   yoghurt
2 fl oz (50 ml) wine vinegar
1 teaspoon honey
salt and black pepper to taste
1 medium pomegranate

Separately, lightly cook the courgettes and green beans in boiling
salted water for 2–3 minutes, then drain, rinse under cold water and
combine with the apple. Mix together the oil, yoghurt, wine vinegar,
honey and salt and pepper to form a dressing and pour this over the
vegetables and apple. Toss together. Cut the pomegranate across
laterally and break out the seeds over the salad, taking care not to
include any bitter skin. Serve.

Basil Tomato Salad
(*Ensalada de Jitomate con Albahaca*)

BRAZIL

Serves 4

1 clove garlic, peeled and
  crushed
3 tablespoons (45 ml) Basic
  Vinaigrette Dressing (see
  page 82)
1 tablespoon (15 ml) finely
  chopped fresh basil

4 medium firm tomatoes,
  sliced
1 medium onion, peeled and
  thinly sliced
salt and black pepper to taste

Combine the garlic, vinaigrette and basil. Arrange the tomato and
onion slices on a serving plate and season with salt and black pepper.
Pour over the dressing and serve.

Roast Bell Pepper Salad
(*Ensalada de Pimientos Asados*)

Serves 6

2 each of red, yellow and green
  bell peppers, left whole but
  pierced 3 times near the
  stem end
2 medium onions, cross-cut
  nearly to base into 6 or 8

1 × 12 oz (350 g) aubergine,
  halved lengthwise
¼ pint (150 ml) olive oil
salt and ground black pepper

Preheat the oven to 475°F (240°C, gas mark 9). Put the peppers and
other prepared vegetables into a large roasting tin and bake in the
oven for 35–45 minutes, turning half way through, until soft, blistered, wrinkled and dark. Skin the onion and break the flesh into
segments. Slice the aubergine into half moons. Arrange both vegetables on a shallow serving dish. Skin the peppers and slice into strips
and arrange with the other vegetables. Drizzle over the oil, season
and serve.

Red Bell Pepper Salad
(*Ensalada de Pimientos Rojos*)

Serves 4

This is good with boiled or baked potatoes.

6 red bell peppers
2 cloves garlic
1 large beefsteak tomato
salt

3 tablespoons (45 ml) olive oil
2 teaspoons wine vinegar
chopped parsley, to garnish

Preheat the oven to 400°F (200°C, gas mark 6). Place the peppers, garlic and tomato in a roasting tin and bake uncovered for 25 minutes. Remove the tomato, then skin and chop it, reserving any juices. Turn the peppers over and return the peppers and garlic to the oven for a further 20 minutes. Skin the peppers, reserving any juices, and slice. Crush the garlic and the tomato with some salt using a pestle and mortar or in a blender. Add the oil, reserved juices and vinegar and mix thoroughly to make a dressing. Arrange the pepper slices in a serving dish and pour the dressing over. Garnish with parsley and serve.

Corn and Red Bean Salad   BOLIVIA
(*Ensalada de Maíz y Judías Rojas*)

Serves 4

4 oz (100 g) dried red kidney
  beans, soaked overnight in
  cold water, or 8 oz (225 g)
  tinned red kidney beans,
  drained
8 oz (225 g) fresh or frozen
  sweetcorn, freshly cooked
1 small onion or shallot,
  peeled and finely sliced

salt to taste
2 tinned plum tomatoes,
  gently pressed free of juice
4 tablespoons (60 ml)
  vegetable oil
2 teaspoons hot chilli sauce

If using dried beans, drain them, cover with fresh water, bring to the boil and boil hard for 10 minutes. Reduce the heat to a simmer, cover, and cook for about 1–1½ hours, until the beans are tender. Drain and allow to cool. Alternatively, use tinned beans.

Stir the beans, sweetcorn and onion together in a salad bowl, lightly season with salt. Combine the tomatoes, vegetable oil and chilli sauce in a mixing bowl and whisk together to make a dressing. Toss the vegetables in the dressing and serve.

Avocado and Red Bean Salad MEXICO
(*Ensalada de Aguacate y Judías Rojas*)

Serves 4

Partially crushed beans covered in an avocado cream form the basis of this salad. Serve with crusty bread or corn chips.

4 oz (100 g) dried red kidney beans, soaked overnight in cold water, or 8 oz (225 g) tinned red kidney beans, drained
1 large avocado
1 clove garlic, peeled and crushed
1 red or green chilli pepper, seeded and finely diced
1 tablespoon (15 ml) olive oil
1 tablespoon (15 ml) lemon juice
salt and black pepper to taste
1 small onion or shallot, peeled and finely sliced
1 bell pepper, seeded and finely cut into rings
2 hard-boiled eggs, shelled and sliced
paprika to taste

If using dried beans, drain them, cover with fresh water, bring to the boil and boil rapidly for 10 minutes. Reduce the heat to a simmer, cover and cook for about 1–1½ hours, until the beans are tender. Drain and allow to cool. Alternatively, use tinned beans. Halve the avocado, remove the stone and scoop out the flesh. Add to it the garlic, chilli pepper, oil, lemon juice and seasoning in a bowl. Mash and stir the mixture to a smooth consistency. Semi-crush the beans, leaving some semblance of their shape, and spoon on to a serving plate. Spoon over the avocado cream and decorate with the onion, bell pepper and egg slices. Sprinkle a little paprika over the top and serve.

Bean and Vegetable Salad
(*Ensalada de Judías y Legumbres*)

Serves 4–6

1 lb (450 g) cooked kidney or
pinto beans or chickpeas
(see page 12 or use tinned
beans)
1 large bell pepper, seeded and
finely chopped
1 medium onion, peeled and
finely sliced
8 oz (225 g) green beans,
cooked and cut into 2 in
(5 cm) lengths

salt, chilli powder and sugar to
taste
3 fl oz (75 ml) wine vinegar or
cider vinegar
4 fl oz (100 ml) olive or
sunflower oil

Combine the beans and all the vegetables in a large serving bowl.
Season to taste with salt (about 1½ teaspoons), chilli powder (about
½ teaspoon) and sugar (about 3 teaspoons). Combine the vinegar
and oil and stir into the salad. Serve immediately or preferably after
chilling in the refrigerator (the longer the better, up to 24 hours after
preparation).

Chayote Salad (*Ensalada de Chayote*)

Serves 4

Cooked chayote (see page 54), chilled and served with hard-boiled
egg and a vinaigrette dressing, makes an unusual and tasty salad.

2 chayote, peeled, seeded and
chopped
1 clove garlic, peeled and
crushed
salt and black pepper to taste
1 hard-boiled egg, shelled and
chopped

½ recipe quantity Basic
Vinaigrette Dressing (see
page 82)
1 tablespoon (15 ml) finely
chopped fresh parsley

Put the chayote in a pan, cover with water, add the garlic, salt and
pepper and bring to the boil. Reduce the heat and simmer for 6–7
minutes or until just tender. Drain. Place the chayote in a serving bowl
and leave, covered, in the refrigerator for 1 hour or more. Stir in the
egg, then the vinaigrette and finally garnish with the parsley. Serve.

Quinoa Mixed Salad
(*Ensalada Mixta de Quinoa*)

Serves 4

This salad improves with chilling, so make it ahead of the time required. Quinoa is a nutritious quick-to-cook grain-like food, originally cultivated in Peru (see page 20).

8 oz (225 g) quinoa
1 medium bell pepper, seeded and finely chopped
2 cloves garlic, peeled and finely chopped
1–2 medium onions, peeled and finely chopped
2 sticks celery, trimmed and finely chopped
1 fresh chilli pepper, seeded and finely chopped (optional)

2 oz (50 g) raisins, plumped up in a little hot water then drained
juice of 1 lemon
2 tablespoons (30 ml) vegetable oil
salt and black pepper to taste

Cover the quinoa in cold water in a pan. Bring to the boil, reduce the heat and simmer for 10 minutes or until tender. Drain and place in a serving bowl. Add the bell pepper, garlic, onions, celery, chilli pepper (if used) and raisins. Mix well. Combine the lemon juice and oil and pour over the salad. Add salt and black pepper to taste and toss well. Chill before serving.

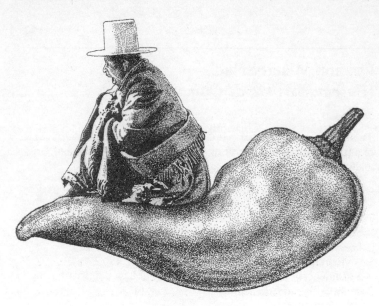

Vegetable Dishes

Vegetable dishes are an important part of Latin American cuisine. Traditionally they would be served separately, either before or after the main course, but nowadays, more and more, they are served alongside or as a main dish in themselves.

Corn, tomatoes, chillies, potatoes, avocados, green beans, onions, garlic, green and red bell peppers, courgettes, aubergines, cabbages, squash and many more familiar vegetables are the basic ingredients of these dishes. However, the Latin American market or vegetable store is a cornucopia not only of these vegetables but of a bewildering array of other more unfamiliar varieties and we have included a few recipes using ingredients such as the chayote (see page 54) that may be new to the reader.

The recipes given here were chosen for their accessibility to the European or North American cook and for their ease of preparation.

Aubergine Casserole (*Cacerola de Berenjena*)

NICARAGUA

Serves 4 as a main dish, 8 as a side dish

Serve with baked potatoes or, for authenticity, baked sweet potatoes (see page 20).

1½ lb (750 g) aubergines, sliced ½ in (1.2 cm) thick
salt
1 tablespoon (15 ml) olive oil
1 medium onion, peeled and finely chopped
2 cloves garlic, peeled and crushed
1 bell pepper, seeded and finely chopped

1–2 green chilli peppers, seeded and finely chopped
1 teaspoon ground cumin
6 tablespoons (90 ml) tomato purée
6 fl oz (175 ml) water
8 oz (225 g) Cheddar cheese, grated
salt and black pepper to taste

Place the aubergine slices in a colander, sprinkle with salt and set aside for 30 minutes. Then rinse under a cold tap and pat dry with absorbent kitchen paper. Preheat the oven to 400°F (200°C, gas mark 6). Place the aubergine slices in a single layer on a greased baking sheet and place in the oven to bake for 10 minutes. Remove and set aside. Leave the oven on for later use. Meanwhile heat the oil in a pan and sauté the onion and garlic until just softened, add the chopped bell pepper and cook for a further 2 minutes. Add the chilli peppers, cumin and tomato purée and cook, stirring, for another 2 minutes. Add the water, bring the mixture to the boil, stirring, then reduce the heat and simmer uncovered for 10 minutes. Place a layer of half the aubergine slices in the bottom of a greased ovenproof dish. Pour over half the sauce and sprinkle half the cheese on top. Repeat with the remaining ingredients and bake in the hot oven for 20 minutes or until nicely browned and cooked through. Serve immediately.

Stuffed Chayotes (*Chayotes Rellenos*) CHILE

Serves 4 as a main dish, 8 as a side dish

The chayote is a pear-shaped member of the squash family, about 5 in (12.5 cm) in length. The colour varies from yellow to dark green, although the most common colour is pale green. The flesh is crunchy in texture and bland in flavour, while the seeds are nutty and crunchy. Chayotes are very popular in Chile, Mexico and many other Latin American countries. They are eaten blanched in salads, cooked on their own or often with sweetcorn, tomatoes and chilli peppers, or stuffed as in the recipe given here. Chayotes are also used in the preparation of sweet tarts and pies.

3 medium chayotes, washed
salt
1 tablespoon (15 ml) vegetable oil
1 large onion, peeled and finely chopped
2 cloves garlic, peeled and crushed
2 large tomatoes, skinned (see page 19) and chopped
1 green or red chilli pepper, seeded and finely chopped

4 oz (100 g) frozen or tinned sweetcorn
1 tablespoon (15 ml) finely chopped fresh oregano or 1 teaspoon dried oregano
black pepper to taste
3 tablespoons (45 ml) fresh breadcrumbs
3 tablespoons (45 ml) grated Parmesan cheese

Boil the chayotes in salted water for 30 minutes or until barely tender. Drain then cut them in half and scoop out and reserve the flesh and seeds, leaving a ½ in (1.2 cm) shell. Heat the oil in a frying pan and sauté the onion and garlic until softened and golden. Add the tomatoes, chilli pepper, sweetcorn, oregano and salt and black pepper to taste. Stir well, heat through and remove from the heat. Stir in the chayote flesh and seeds. Fill the chayote shells with this mixture. Top with the breadcrumbs and the Parmesan cheese and brown under a hot grill. Serve immediately.

Courgettes Stuffed with Corn and Egg (*Calabacitas Rellenas de Elote y Huevos*)   GUATEMALA

Serves 4

This is a filling main course dish.

2 lb (900 g) large courgettes
salt
1 tablespoon (15 ml) vegetable oil
1 medium onion, peeled and finely chopped
1–2 fresh green or red chilli peppers, seeded and chopped

12 oz (350 g) fresh or frozen sweetcorn
2 large eggs
4 tablespoons (60 ml) double cream
3 oz (75 g) Parmesan cheese, finely grated

Cut the stem ends off the courgettes and carefully hollow out the centre of each with an apple corer leaving an ⅛–¼ in (0.3–0.6 cm) shell. Discard the pulp. Soak the courgette shells in salted water for 10 minutes, then drain them off and set aside. Preheat the oven to 350°F (180°C, gas mark 4). Heat the oil in a pan, add the onion and chilli pepper and sauté until just softened. Transfer to a blender or food processor and add the remaining ingredients. Blend to a smooth, thick texture. Stuff the courgette shells with this mixture and lay in a greased baking dish. Bake in the preheated oven for 35 minutes. Serve immediately.

Courgettes with Pepper and Cream Sauce (*Calabacitas con Salsa de Rajas y Crema*)   MEXICO

Serves 4 as a main dish, 8 as a side dish

The squash family is native to Mexico and courgettes are a particular favourite.

6 green bell peppers
2 medium onions, peeled and
    finely chopped
2 cloves garlic, peeled and
    finely chopped
4 tablespoons (60 ml)
    vegetable oil
8 fl oz (225 ml) water
2 lb (900 g) small courgettes,
    cut into ½ in (1.2 cm)
    rounds

salt and black pepper to taste
6 fl oz (175 ml) double cream
    or crème fraîche (for a
    lighter dish)
8 oz (225 g) Cheddar cheese,
    grated

Grill and skin the peppers (see page 13). Cut them open, remove the seeds and chop coarsely. Put the peppers, onions and garlic in a blender and purée into a smooth paste. Heat the oil in a large pan and cook the paste for 3 minutes over a low heat, stirring constantly. Add the water, courgettes and seasoning. Stir well, cover and simmer over a very low heat for 30 minutes or until the courgettes are tender. Add a little water if the mixture gets too dry. Stir in the cream or crème fraîche and heat through. Serve immediately, topped with the grated cheese.

Green Vegetables (*Verduras Verdes*)

Serves 4–6 as a side dish

A side dish of green vegetables may be served with any savoury meal. Broccoli, kale, chard, green cabbage or spinach are suitable ingredients for this recipe.

3 tablespoons (45 ml) olive oil
1 medium onion, peeled and
    finely chopped
2 cloves garlic, peeled and
    crushed

1½ lb (750 g) greens (see
    above), chopped or
    shredded, washed and
    drained

Heat the oil in a heavy frying pan or large saucepan over a medium heat. Add the onion and garlic and sauté until just coloured. Add the greens and cook with regular stirring until just softened, about 5 minutes. Serve immediately.

Cabbage in Wine Sauce (*Repôlho com Vinho*)

BRAZIL

Serves 4 as a side dish

Green, white and red cabbage are all popular in Latin America. Coleslaw salad is as ubiquitous as it is in America and Europe and sauerkraut is widely eaten. This recipe gives a more interesting and tasty way of preparing this universal vegetable. It is good with baked potatoes topped with cheese.

1 small head white or green cabbage
salt
2 tablespoons (30 ml) vegetable oil
1 medium onion, peeled and finely chopped
1 fresh green or red chilli pepper, seeded and chopped
1 red or green bell pepper, seeded and chopped

3 tablespoons (45 ml) finely chopped fresh parsley
1 × 8 oz (225 g) can of plum tomatoes, drained and chopped
6 fl oz (175 ml) dry white wine
2 fl oz (50 ml) water
black pepper to taste

Wash the cabbage and shred it finely. Drop it into a large saucepan of boiling salted water, bring back to the boil and simmer for 5 minutes. Drain thoroughly and set aside in the pan. Heat the oil in another saucepan and sauté the onion, chilli pepper, bell pepper and parsley until the onion is softened and starting to colour. Add the remaining ingredients, including salt to taste. Stir and bring to the boil. Pour over the cabbage, return to the boil, reduce the heat, cover and simmer for 5 minutes. Serve immediately.

Variation To make the dish more substantial, add 1 lb (450 g) cooked and chopped potatoes to the cabbage before adding the remaining ingredients. This is a Bolivian variation of the dish.

Chard with Chilli Cream Sauce (*Acelgas con Crema*)

MEXICO

Serves 4 as a side dish

Chard leaves are dark green and spinach-like, but their flavour is mild. The stalks are broad and white in colour, with a stronger flavour than the leaf. In this dish, cooked chard, leaf and stalk, is served in a chilli-hot cream sauce. Serve as an accompaniment to less rich vegetable or grain dishes.

1½ lb (750 g) chard, washed and drained
salt
1–2 fresh green or red chilli peppers, seeded
8 fl oz (225 ml) double cream

1 tablespoon (15 ml) vegetable oil
1 small onion, peeled and finely chopped
black pepper to taste

Cut the leaves off the stalks of the chard and cook the stalks in a pan of salted boiling water for 3 minutes, now add the leaves and cook for a further minute. Drain and rinse the leaves and stalks under cold water. Drain again and coarsely chop the leaves and stalks. Put the chilli pepper and cream in a blender and, in short bursts, process until smooth. Heat the oil in a pan, add the onion and sauté until soft. Add the cream sauce and cook, stirring, over a low heat until very hot but not boiling. Stir in the chard leaves and stalks, season to taste, heat through and serve.

Variation Substitute spinach for the chard.

Toasted Cassava Meal (*Farofa*)

Makes 8 oz (225 g)

Toasted cassava meal (also called manioc) is served as a seasoning throughout Latin America. Shakers of it are often found on restaurant tables. Slightly crunchy and mildly sour, it is sprinkled over a variety of foods, especially bean dishes. Sometimes it is fried with palm oil (butter may be used as a substitute) before being used.

8 oz (225 g) cassava meal

4 tablespoons (60 ml) palm oil (dende) or melted butter (optional)

Toast the cassava meal in a heavy frying pan over a low heat, stirring constantly, until it turns a pale brown colour. Add the palm oil or melted butter, if using, and stir until well blended. Transfer to a small bowl and spoon over food as you wish.

Cassava Root with Cheese Sauce (*Picante de Yuca*)   PERU

Serves 4 as a main dish, 8 as a side dish

The sauce for this dish is very hot, so reduce the number of chilli peppers used if you prefer a milder dish.

2 lb (900 g) cassava root, peeled and sliced
salt
8 oz (225 g) Cheddar cheese, grated
8 fl oz (225 ml) olive oil or other vegetable oil

5 red or green chilli peppers, seeded and finely chopped
black pepper to taste
2 hard-boiled eggs, shelled and sliced
green olives, to garnish

Boil the cassava root in salted water until tender, about 25–30 minutes. Meanwhile, blend together the cheese, oil and chilli peppers until smooth, then season to taste. Heat this sauce through very gently if you want it hot. Drain the cooked cassava, arrange the slices on a serving dish and pour over the sauce. Top with slices of egg, garnish with olives and serve immediately.

Variations The cassava root could be replaced by corn on the cob, cauliflower, potatoes or other vegetables.

Corn on the Cob (*Choclo Sancochado*)

Serves 4 as a side dish

Buy the freshest corn you can. To test for freshness, press one of the kernels: if it spurts juice it's fresh. Corn with smallish, firm but milky kernels is the best.

METHOD 1: BOILED

The following recipe gives the simplest and one of the best ways of preparing corn on the cob. Serve the corn with a good size knob of butter. Salt is normally added after cooking the cobs, otherwise it toughens the kernels.

4 ears of sweetcorn	butter
water	salt to taste (optional)

If the corn hasn't already been stripped, remove the husks and silk (to remove the silk, hold the ear of corn under a cold running tap and brush with a soft vegetable brush). Bring a large pan of water to the boil (there should be enough water to just cover all the ears of corn) and then drop in the corn. Return the water to the boil and cook the corn for 4–6 minutes or until tender. Drain and serve with a knob of butter. Sprinkle with a little salt if desired.

METHOD 2: STEAMED

Another way to cook the corn is to steam it over a bed of husks. Buy the corn cobs in their husks, strip these off and use them to cover the bottom of a large pan. Add enough water to come halfway up the bed of husks. Bring to the boil. Arrange the corn cobs on the bed of husks, tightly cover the pan, and steam the corn for 3–5 minutes. Again, serve with a knob of butter and a sprinkling of salt if desired.

METHOD 3: BAKED

This method is an excellent way of preparing corn on the cob both at home and out-of-doors on camping trips or at a barbecue, when a wood fire or charcoal grill is used in place of the oven.

4 ears of sweetcorn in their husks	salt to taste
1 tablespoon (15 ml) vegetable oil or melted butter	

Preheat the oven to 425°F (220°C, gas mark 7). Open the ears of corn by gently turning back the husks. Remove the silk and then brush each ear with the oil or melted butter, and sprinkle with salt to taste. Replace the husks, place the cobs on a baking tray and bake in the preheated oven until tender, about 15 minutes. To cook on a fire, allow the flames to die down and place the corn cobs, prepared as above, on the hot embers. Keep turning them and bake for 15–20 minutes.

Puréed Corn (*Humitas*) ARGENTINA

Serves 4 as a side dish

Here sweetcorn kernels are puréed with milk and cooked with pumpkin and cheese. Serve as an accompaniment to other dishes.

1 lb (450 g) fresh or frozen
  sweetcorn
5 tablespoons (75 ml) milk
salt, black pepper and chilli
  sauce to taste
1 oz (25 g) butter
1 small onion, peeled and
  diced

4 oz (100 g) pumpkin or other
  squash, cut into 1 in
  (2.5 cm) cubes
2 oz (50 g) Parmesan cheese,
  finely grated

Put the corn kernels, milk and seasonings in a blender or food processor and purée. Heat the butter in a pan and sauté the onion and pumpkin until softened and tender. Add the corn purée and mix well. Cook over a low heat, stirring, until heated through. Stir in the cheese, quickly transfer to a serving dish and serve immediately.

Corn Casserole (*Cacerola de Maíz*)

Serves 4

This thick, filling, quick-to-prepare casserole dish contains all the basic ingredients of Latin American cooking – cornmeal, bell peppers, tomatoes, beans, onions, chillies and cheese. Serve with a green salad, tortillas (see page 85) and Salsa Cruda or Salsa Fresca (see page 75).

4 oz (100 g) cornmeal
1½ pints (900 ml) water
1 teaspoon salt
2 tablespoons (30 ml)
  vegetable oil
1 medium green or red bell
  pepper, seeded and chopped
1 medium onion, peeled and
  chopped
2 cloves garlic, peeled and
  crushed
2 fresh or dried red or green
  chilli peppers, seeded and
  chopped

12 oz (350 g) ripe tomatoes,
  skinned (see page 19) and
  chopped
12 oz (350 g) cooked kidney or
  pinto beans (use tinned
  beans or soak 5 oz (150 g)
  dried beans overnight, drain,
  cover with fresh water and
  cook until tender – see page
  12)
2 oz (50 g) Cheddar cheese,
  grated

Combine the cornmeal, water and half the salt in a saucepan and
gently bring to the boil, stirring constantly. Reduce the heat to low
and simmer for 15 minutes, stirring often. In another pan, heat the
oil and sauté the bell pepper, onion, garlic and chilli peppers until
softened. Stir in the tomatoes, beans and remaining salt and simmer
for 10 minutes. Meanwhile, preheat the oven to 350°F (180°C, gas
mark 4). Grease an ovenproof casserole dish and spread half the
cooked cornmeal in the bottom. Cover with the vegetable and bean
mixture, top with the remaining cornmeal and sprinkle over the
cheese. Bake in the oven for 25 minutes or until the cheese has just
started to brown. Serve.

Mushrooms in Green Sauce   MEXICO
(*Hongos en Salsa Verde*)

Serves 4 as a side dish

The green sauce is authentically made with small green tomatoes
called tomatillos. Even when ripe they are firm with a tart flavour.
They are much used in Mexican cooking. Gooseberries make an
almost perfect substitute.

2 tablespoons (30 ml)
  vegetable oil
1 small onion, peeled and
  finely sliced
12 oz (350 g) mushrooms,
  wiped and coarsely chopped
2 fresh green or red chilli
  peppers, seeded and
  chopped

¼ teaspoon ground cumin seed
8 oz (225 g) fresh or tinned
  green tomatoes (tomatillos)
  or gooseberries
1 clove garlic, peeled and
  crushed
salt to taste

Heat the oil in a large frying pan, add the onion and sauté until softened. Add the mushrooms and chilli peppers and briefly stir-fry. Blend together the cumin seed, green tomatoes or gooseberries and garlic in a blender or food processor and pour over the mushrooms. Season with salt and stir well. Cover and gently simmer for 20 minutes or until the mushrooms are tender.

Creamed Mushrooms and Green Peppers (*Hongos y Poblanos con Crema*)

Serves 4

Serve as a vegetable side dish or for a light meal on its own on toast or warm tortillas.

2 oz (50 g) butter
6 oz (175 g) mushrooms,
  wiped and sliced
1 small green bell pepper,
  seeded and finely chopped
1 small onion, peeled and
  finely chopped
1½ tablespoons (25 ml)
  cornflour

salt to taste
pinch of grated nutmeg
¾ pint (450 ml) milk, hot
1 egg yolk
2 fl oz (50 ml) crème fraîche or
  cream
cayenne pepper to taste

Melt the butter in a frying pan and sauté the mushrooms, bell pepper and onion until softened. Stir in the cornflour, salt to taste and nutmeg. Slowly stir in the milk and continue to stir until the mixture thickens and is coming to a boil. Reduce the heat to very low. Beat the egg yolk and crème fraîche or cream together and then stir into the pan. Cook for 1–2 minutes, then serve, garnished with a sprinkling of cayenne pepper to taste.

Stuffed Peppers in Walnut Sauce   MEXICO
(*Chiles en Nogada*)

Serves 6

This rich colourful dish of red, white and green (the colours of the
Mexican flag) is traditionally served in Mexico on Independence
Day (15 September). It is eaten hot or cold.

FILLING

2 tablespoons (30 ml)
  vegetable oil
1 medium onion, peeled and
  finely chopped
1 clove garlic, peeled and
  crushed
1 chilli pepper, seeded and
  finely chopped
1 × 8 oz (225 g) can of
  tomatoes, drained
2 oz (50 g) sultanas
3 oz (75 g) chopped almonds
1 medium cooking apple,
  peeled, cored and diced
1 lb (450 g) cooked rice or
  refried beans (see page 107)

PEPPERS

2 eggs, separated
flour
6 green bell peppers, tops cut
  off, cored, seeded, washed
  and dried
vegetable oil for frying
SAUCE
4 oz (100 g) walnuts, finely
  ground
8 oz (225 g) cream cheese
½ pint (275 ml) single cream
½ teaspoon ground cinnamon
2 teaspoons sugar
GARNISH
seeds from 1 small
  pomegranate

Preheat the oven to 350°F (180°C, gas mark 4), then prepare the
filling. Heat the oil in a large pan and sauté the onion and garlic until
just softened and colouring. Add the chilli pepper, tomatoes, sultanas, almonds and apple, cover and simmer for 10 minutes. Stir in
the rice or beans and set aside.

To prepare the peppers, whisk the egg whites until stiff, then beat
the yolks gently and fold them into the whites. Sprinkle some flour
on to a worktop and roll the peppers in it, then dip each into the egg
mixture to coat the outside surface. Pour ½ in (1.2 cm) vegetable oil
into a large pan and heat over a moderate heat.

Cook the peppers, 2 at a time, in the hot oil until the egg coating has
cooked and coloured. Drain them, pat off excess oil with absorbent
kitchen paper and stand in a greased ovenproof dish. Fill them with
the filling, placing excess in the bottom of the dish. Cover with a lid
or foil and bake in the preheated oven for 20 minutes. Arrange on a
serving dish.

To make the sauce, put all the ingredients except half the cream into a blender, or use a bowl and whisk, and beat into a smooth sauce. Add more cream as required, but aim to produce a thick sauce. Heat the sauce very gently (do not boil) if the dish is to be served hot. Pour the sauce over the peppers. Cut the pomegranate across laterally and break out the seeds over the top of the dish, taking care not to include any bitter skin.

Baked Pineapple (*Abacaxi Assarbo*) BRAZIL

Serves 6 as a side dish

Here is a simple-to-prepare and unusual side dish to accompany rice and bean dishes.

1 whole pineapple, top cut off

Preheat the oven to 350°F (180°C, gas mark 4). Place the pineapple, upright, in an ovenproof dish in the oven and bake for 45 minutes. Remove, cut into 6 thick slices and serve. Eat with a knife and fork or use your hands.

Lentils with Pineapple and Plantain MEXICO (*Lentejas con Piña y Plátano*)

Serves 4 as a main dish, 8 as a side dish

With an unusual but winning combination of flavours, the sweetness of this dish is often enjoyed by children.

6 oz (175 g) brown or green lentils
2½ pints (1.5 litres) water
2 tablespoons (30 ml) vegetable oil
1 small onion, peeled and finely chopped
1 clove garlic, peeled and finely chopped

1 large tomato, skinned (see page 19) and chopped
8 oz (225 g) fresh or tinned pineapple pieces
8 oz (225 g) very ripe plantains, peeled and cut into thin slices
salt to taste

Put the lentils and water into a pan, bring to the boil, cover, lower the heat and simmer until tender, about 1–1½ hours. Drain and reserve the liquid. Heat the oil in a heavy frying pan and sauté the onion and garlic until softened. Add the tomato and cook briskly over a high heat, stirring constantly, until the mixture is reduced to a thick sauce consistency. Reduce the heat and add the pineapple and plantain. Gently heat through and then stir in the lentils and reserved liquid, made up if necessary to 12 fl oz (350 ml) with water. Season to taste with salt. Cook over a low heat, stirring occasionally, for 15 minutes and serve.

Fried Plantain (*Llantén Frito*)

Serves 4 as a side dish

Green plantain chips cooked in this way are good as an appetizer with drinks, while ripe plantain prepared in the same manner is served as a side dish, and fried overripe plantain chips, sprinkled with sugar and cinnamon, become a dessert.

3 plantains	salt and paprika or pepper *or*
vegetable oil for frying	sugar and cinnamon to taste

Cut both ends off the plantains. Slit the skins lengthways right through to the flesh and prise off. Cut each plantain into three, crossways, and then slice thickly along the length. Heat the vegetable oil until moderately hot in a heavy frying pan (containing 2–3 in (5–7 cm) oil) and fry the plantain slices until tender and golden brown, about 5 minutes. Drain on absorbent kitchen paper and serve very hot, seasoned or sugared to taste.

Boiled Plantain (*Llantén Cocido*)

Serves 4 as a side dish

salt	4–6 unripe green plantains

Bring a large pan of salted water to the boil. Cut off both ends of the plantains and using a sharp knife score the skins deeply along their length. Either leave the plantains whole or cut in two crossways. Boil for 20 minutes until the plantains are soft. Drain. When cool enough to handle, remove the skins and serve.

Plantain and Lime Torte
(*Torta de Llantén y Lima*)

Serves 4

Serve this simple and filling egg dish with rice.

salt
2 lb (900 g) green plantains
3 large eggs
juice of 1 lime
2 tablespoons (30 ml) fresh
   breadcrumbs

1 red bell pepper, seeded and
   sliced
1 oz (25 g) butter

Bring a large pan of salted water to the boil. Cut off both ends of the plantains and using a sharp knife score the skins deeply along their length. Either leave the plantains whole or cut in two crossways. Boil for 20 minutes until the plantains are soft. Drain. When cool enough to handle, remove the skins and cut into slices. Preheat the oven to 350°F (180°C, gas mark 4). Beat the eggs in a bowl and add the lime juice and plantain slices. Transfer the mixture to a 2½ pint (1.5 litre) soufflé dish or ring mould. Sprinkle breadcrumbs over the top, then decorate with bell pepper rings and dot with butter. Bake in the preheated oven for 1 hour or until a skewer inserted into the torte comes out clean and the top is browned.

Pumpkin Stew (*Locro*)   PERU

Serves 4

Locro is a popular vegetable stew or thick soup made across the countries of Latin America. The main vegetable ingredient may differ, although potato is a popular choice. In this recipe we use pumpkin, but other varieties of squash could be substituted.

3 lb (1.4 kg) pumpkin or other
   squash
3 tablespoons (45 ml) olive oil
2 medium onions, peeled and
   finely chopped
2 cloves garlic, peeled and
   crushed
2 large tomatoes, skinned (see
   page 19) and chopped
4 fl oz (100 ml) water

2 tablespoons (30 ml) finely
   chopped fresh oregano or
   2 teaspoons dried oregano
salt and black pepper to taste
8 oz (225 g) fresh or frozen
   sweetcorn
4 oz (100 g) fresh or frozen
   green peas
8 oz (225 g) feta cheese, cut
   into tiny cubes

Cut open the pumpkin and remove and discard the seeds and
stringy bits. Remove the peel, then cut the flesh into small cubes,
about 1 in (2.5 cm) in size, and set aside. In a large pan, heat the oil
and sauté the onions and garlic until softened and golden. Add the
pumpkin, tomatoes, water, oregano and salt and black pepper to
taste. Cover and cook over a low heat, stirring now and again, until
the pumpkin is almost tender. Now add the sweetcorn and cook for
a further 5 minutes. Add the peas and cook for a further 2–3 minutes
until heated through. Serve garnished with the feta cheese cubes.

Baked Sweet Potatoes (*Camotes Asados*)

Serves 4 as a side dish

Sweet potatoes are used a lot in South American cooking. On their
own, they are served baked or fried (see below) as an accompaniment to a main dish or with a salad as a light meal in themselves.
Both the variety with reddish purple skin and white flesh and the
one with reddish brown skin and orange flesh are used.

4 sweet potatoes, washed   vegetable oil
   (scrubbed if dirty) and dried

Preheat the oven to 400°F (200°C, gas mark 6). Rub the sweet potatoes all over with oil and place in a baking tin. Put in the oven and
bake for 45 minutes to 1 hour or until a fork pushed into them
pierces easily into the middle.

Fried Sweet Potatoes (*Camotes Fritos*)

Serves 4–6 as a side dish

3 sweet potatoes, washed
  (scrubbed if dirty) and dried

vegetable oil for frying
salt to taste

Cut the sweet potatoes into strips lengthwise, about ⅛ in (3 mm) thick. Heat about 5 in (12.5 cm) of oil in a deep pan to 375°F (190°C) and place the sweet potato slices, a few at a time, into the hot oil. Fry until lightly browned, about 2–3 minutes. Remove from the oil, drain on absorbent kitchen paper and serve hot, sprinkled with salt to taste.

Baked Sweet Potato with Apple (*Camote con Fruta*)

Serves 4 as a main dish, 8 as a side dish

The sweetness of this dish will be particularly appreciated when served as an accompaniment to chilli-hot dishes, or try it as a main dish with rice, beans and Salsa Fresca (see page 75).

1 lb (450 g) sweet potatoes,
  washed (scrubbed if dirty),
  dried and sliced
salt
8 oz (225 g) firm green eating
  apples, cored and sliced
juice of 3 medium-sized
  oranges or 6 fl oz (175 ml)
  orange juice

juice of 1 lime
1 oz (25 g) butter
3 tablespoons (45 ml) brown
  sugar
cinnamon to taste

Place the sweet potato slices in a pan of boiling salted water and cook gently for 3–4 minutes. Drain and set aside. Preheat the oven to 350°F (180°C, gas mark 4). In a greased shallow baking dish make alternate layers of sweet potato and apple slices. Pour over the orange and lime juice. Dot the top with butter, sprinkle over the sugar and cinnamon to taste and bake in the preheated oven for 30 minutes or until tender and browned.

Potatoes with Cheese Sauce (*Papas Charreadas*)

COLOMBIA

Serves 4 as a main dish, 8 as a side dish

6 medium potatoes
salt
1 tablespoon (15 ml) vegetable
  oil or butter
1 medium onion, peeled and
  finely chopped
1 lb (450 g) tomatoes,
  skinned, seeded (see page
  19) and chopped

black pepper to taste
2 fl oz (50 ml) double cream
4 oz (100 g) Cheddar cheese,
  grated

Cook the potatoes in their skins in boiling salted water until tender. Drain. Meanwhile, heat the oil or butter in a frying pan and sauté the onion until softened. Add the tomatoes and salt and black pepper to taste. Stir and simmer the mixture until blended together. Reduce the heat, stir in the cream and grated cheese and cook until the cheese melts. Peel the potatoes, pour over the sauce and serve.

Potato Casserole (*Entomatodo de Papas*) PERU

Serves 4 as a main dish, 8 as a side dish

1 large onion, peeled and
  finely sliced
1 clove garlic, peeled and
  finely chopped
2 tablespoons (30 ml) finely
  chopped fresh thyme or 2
  teaspoons dried thyme
salt
2 lb (900 g) potatoes, peeled
  and sliced about ⅛ in
  (3 mm) thick

1 lb (450 g) Mozzarella or
  Cheddar cheese, grated
2 fresh red or green chilli
  peppers, seeded and finely
  chopped
1 lb (450 g) tomatoes, thickly
  sliced
3 oz (75 g) chopped almonds
2 tablespoons (30 ml)
  vegetable oil

Preheat the oven to 375°F (190°C, gas mark 5). Cover the bottom of a greased casserole or baking dish with the sliced onion and sprinkle over the garlic, one third of the thyme and ½ teaspoon salt. Arrange half the potato slices on top and over them sprinkle one third of the cheese, another third of thyme and half the chilli pepper. Cover with tomato slices and sprinkle over ½ teaspoon salt, the remaining thyme and chilli pepper and half the remaining cheese. Cover with the remaining potato slices, sprinkle over the remaining cheese, ½ teaspoon salt and the almonds and drizzle over the oil. Cover with a tight fitting lid or aluminium foil and bake for 1 hour or until the potatoes are just tender. Remove the cover and bake for a further 10 minutes. Serve.

Potatoes Arequipa (*Papas Arequipa*) PERU

Serves 4 as a main dish, 8 as a side dish

The Incas grew many types of potatoes and developed many ways of cooking them. In this traditional dish, cooked potatoes are served in a hot chilli, nut and cheese sauce.

2 lb (900 g) medium potatoes, peeled and halved	1 small onion, peeled and finely sliced
salt	2 cloves garlic, peeled and crushed
2–4 fresh red chilli peppers, seeded and finely chopped	4 oz (100 g) white Cheshire or feta cheese
4 oz (100 g) peanut or hazelnut butter	milk
2 fl oz (50 ml) double cream	4 hard-boiled eggs, shelled and halved
3 fl oz (75 ml) peanut oil or other vegetable oil	12 black olives

Cook the potatoes until just tender in boiling salted water, then drain. Meanwhile, put the chilli peppers, peanut or hazelnut butter, cream and 2 fl oz (50 ml) of the oil into a blender and process to a smooth paste. Sauté the onion and garlic in the remaining oil until softened, then add to the blender together with the cheese. Blend to a smooth consistency and add enough milk to thin the sauce to just pour. Arrange the just-cooked potatoes, cut side down, on a serving dish. Pour the sauce over, garnish with the hard-boiled eggs and olives and serve warm or cold. If you prefer, the sauce can be gently heated before pouring over the potatoes.

Potato Cakes (*Llapingachos*) ECUADOR

Serves 4

Serve this Ecuadorian speciality with a salad of lettuce, tomatoes and avocado slices. For a more substantial dish, top each portion of potato cakes with a fried egg and/or serve with Peanut Sauce (see page 80). Firm floury potatoes produce the firmest potato cakes.

2 lb (900 g) potatoes, peeled
    and thickly sliced
salt
2 medium onions, peeled and
    finely diced

2 oz (50 g) butter
8 oz (225 g) Cheddar cheese,
    grated
vegetable oil for frying

Cook the potatoes until tender in boiling salted water, drain and then mash. Sauté the onions in the butter until well softened. Stir the onions and cheese into the mashed potato and mix well together. Form the mixture into 12 flat patties about 1 in (2.5 cm) thick. Set aside in the refrigerator for 30 minutes (this is not essential if you are in a hurry; it just helps the cakes keep their shape when frying). Shallow-fry the potato cakes, in batches, until golden brown on both sides. Alternatively, place on a greased baking sheet and brown under a grill or on the top shelf of a hot oven.

Egg Moqueca (*Moqueca aos Ovos*) BRAZIL

Serves 4

Moqueca are palm oil-flavoured thick stews, usually made with vegetables and meat or fish, though here we use eggs. Serve with rice and a green vegetable or side salad. If palm oil is unavailable, try using another strongly flavoured oil or more olive oil.

2 tablespoons (30 ml) olive oil
2 medium onions, peeled and
    finely sliced
2 cloves garlic, peeled and
    finely chopped

1 tablespoon (15 ml) finely
    chopped fresh coriander
8 eggs
1 tablespoon (15 ml) palm oil
salt and black pepper to taste

Heat the olive oil in a heavy frying pan and sauté the onion and garlic in it until softened. Add the coriander and continue to cook and stir until the onion is lightly browned. Beat the eggs lightly and then pour them into the pan. Stir and cook until partially set. Drizzle in the palm oil, add salt and black pepper to taste, reduce the heat and cook, stirring occasionally, until set. Serve immediately.

Cheese and Avocado Omelette
(*Tortilla de Queso y Aguacate*)

Serves 2

4 eggs
1 fresh red or green chilli
  pepper, seeded and finely
  chopped
salt and black pepper to taste
vegetable oil or butter for
  frying

4 oz (100 g) Cheddar cheese,
  grated
1 small ripe avocado, halved,
  stoned, peeled and sliced

Beat the eggs, stir in the chilli pepper and season with salt and black pepper. Heat the oil or butter in a frying pan and pour in the eggs. Allow to set a little, then sprinkle over the cheese. Cook until the cheese begins to melt. Arrange the avocado slices over half the omelette. Fold over the other half and serve immediately.

Variation Add 2 oz (50 g) sweetcorn along with the cheese.

Sauces and Salad Dressings

In Mexico and Peru, sauces (*salsas*) are used mainly as table condiments to enliven uncooked or cooked dishes from breakfast to dinner. The sauces, normally chilli-based, are used as dips or added personally to the food to give the degree of hotness required by each diner. In other Latin American cuisines, sauces are more likely to be incorporated into specific dishes and there is no great sauce-making tradition, apart from the tomato- and avocado-based sauces found in many different styles of cooking.

Here we give a selection of sauces that may be served alongside the dishes presented in this book or cooked with them in the more conventional manner. Where the latter is the case for a specific dish, the recipe will refer you to a particular sauce. To simplify matters, we have divided the sauces into three categories: uncooked sauces with chilli peppers, cooked sauces with chilli peppers and sauces without chilli peppers.

UNCOOKED SAUCES WITH CHILLI PEPPERS

Salsa Cruda

Makes 8 fl oz (225 ml)

This simple uncooked chilli sauce goes as naturally with a Mexican meal as salt and pepper does with a typical Western European meal. It is best made at the last minute. The tomatoes do not need to be peeled or seeded.

1 large ripe tomato (about 6 oz (175 g)) or two smaller ones, diced

2 (or more) fresh green chilli peppers, seeded and finely chopped

1 tablespoon (15 ml) finely chopped onion

1 tablespoon (15 ml) finely chopped fresh coriander

1 teaspoon salt or to taste

Combine all the ingredients together, mix well and serve in a small bowl.

Note: Tinned tomatoes are better in this sauce than poor quality (insipid) fresh ones.

Salsa Fresca

Makes 12 fl oz (350 ml)

This is another version of Salsa Cruda (see above).

1 lb (450 g) ripe tomatoes, chopped

½ small onion, peeled and finely diced

1–2 fresh green chilli peppers, seeded and finely chopped

1 tablespoon (15 ml) finely chopped fresh coriander

4 tablespoons (60 ml) red wine vinegar

5 tablespoons (75 ml) water

salt to taste

Combine all the ingredients, mix well and use immediately or store in the refrigerator and use within 2 days.

Chilean Sauce (*Salsa Chilena*)

Makes 8 fl oz (225 ml)

This chilli sauce includes oil and vinegar and uses onion rather than tomato as the base ingredient; consequently it keeps better than Salsa Cruda (see page 75). Make ahead of time and store in the refrigerator until required.

2 (or more) fresh green chilli peppers, seeded and finely chopped
1 tablespoon (15 ml) vegetable oil
1 tablespoon (15 ml) white wine vinegar

4 fl oz (100 ml) water
2 medium onions, peeled and finely chopped
2 tablespoons (30 ml) finely chopped fresh parsley or coriander
1 teaspoon salt or to taste

Place all the ingredients in a blender or food processor and process briefly until the salsa is mixed but not too smooth. Taste and adjust seasonings as necessary.

Brazilian Lime Sauce (*Molho Brasileiro*)

Makes 4 fl oz (100 ml)

This popular sauce is normally served with meats, but it's also good with plain cooked vegetables.

5 tablespoons (75 ml) freshly squeezed lime juice
1 tablespoon (15 ml) finely diced onion
1 tablespoon (15 ml) finely chopped parsley

½ tablespoon (7.5 ml) finely chopped fresh coriander
¼–½ teaspoon chilli sauce
salt and black pepper to taste

Combine all the ingredients in a glass or ceramic bowl. Cover and set aside at room temperature for 30 minutes or more to allow flavours to develop before serving.

COOKED SAUCES WITH CHILLI PEPPERS

Red Chilli Tomato Sauce
(*Salsa de Chiles Rojos*)

Makes ¼ pint (450 ml)

Sauces made with red chilli peppers tend to be hotter than green
chilli sauces, but the ripe red peppers also carry with them a hint of
sweetness.

5 fresh red chilli peppers,
  seeded
1 lb (450 g) large tomatoes,
  grilled until blistered and
  soft
2 cloves garlic, peeled and
  finely chopped

1 medium onion, peeled and
  finely chopped
1 tablespoon (15 ml) vegetable
  oil
salt to taste

Cover the chilli peppers in boiling water and leave for 5 minutes.
Drain and place them in a blender or food processor with the tomatoes, the garlic and the onion. Blend until smooth. Heat the oil in a
saucepan, pour in the tomato mixture, add salt to taste and cook,
stirring, over a moderate heat for 10–15 minutes. Serve hot or leave
the sauce to cool and store in the refrigerator until required.

Green Chilli Tomato Sauce
(*Salsa de Chiles Verdes y Jitomate*)

Makes ¼ pint (450 ml)

1 lb (450 g) tomatoes,
  chopped
1 medium onion, peeled and
  finely chopped
2 fresh green chilli peppers,
  seeded and chopped
2 cloves garlic, peeled and
  finely chopped

salt to taste
1 tablespoon (15 ml) vegetable
  oil
1 tablespoon (15 ml) finely
  chopped fresh coriander

Place the tomatoes, onion, chilli peppers and garlic in a blender or food processor and process briefly until almost smooth (leave a little texture). Season to taste with salt. Heat the oil in a saucepan, add the tomato mixture and cook, stirring, for about 5 minutes or until thickened up. Stir in the coriander. Serve hot or allow to cool and store in the refrigerator until required.

Salsa Fría   COLOMBIA

Makes 1 pint (550 ml)

This sauce uses pineapple to add sweetness and lime juice to balance it with sourness. Try it on cooked rice or vegetables or as a pickle with cheese sandwiches or cheese dishes.

1 tablespoon (15 ml) vegetable oil
1 tablespoon (15 ml) finely chopped onion
1 teaspoon ground cumin
2 (or more) fresh red or green chilli peppers, seeded and finely chopped

1 lb (450 g) fresh or tinned tomatoes, chopped
8 oz (225 g) fresh or tinned (unsweetened) pineapple, finely chopped
juice of 1 lime
salt and black pepper to taste

Heat the oil in a saucepan, add the onion, cumin and chilli peppers and sauté until the onion is softened and just starting to colour. Add the tomatoes, pineapple and lime juice. Cover and very gently simmer for 25 minutes. Season to taste with salt and black pepper. Cool and serve. Store unused sauce in the refrigerator; it will keep for up to a week.

Red Chilli and Paprika Tomato Sauce
(*Salsa de Jitomate con Chiles y Pimienta Roja*)

Makes ¾ pint (450 ml)

This sauce, unlike the others, uses tomato purée rather than fresh tomatoes. It is quick to prepare and good hot or cold.

3–5 fresh red chilli peppers, seeded

2 tablespoons (30 ml) vegetable oil

2 medium onions, peeled and finely chopped

2 cloves garlic, peeled and finely chopped

3 tablespoons (45 ml) tomato purée

2 teaspoons paprika

4 fl oz (100 ml) water or red wine

salt to taste

Cover the chilli peppers in boiling water and leave for 5 minutes. Drain and finely chop them. Heat the oil in a pan and sauté the onion and garlic until starting to colour. Add the chilli peppers, reduce the heat, cover and cook for 10 minutes or until the onions are very soft. Add the tomato purée, paprika and water or wine and simmer, covered, for a further 10 minutes. Add salt to taste. Serve hot or leave the sauce to cool and store in the refrigerator until required.

SAUCES WITHOUT CHILLI PEPPERS

Basic Tomato Sauce

Makes 8 fl oz (225 ml)

This is a basic red sauce. You can make it in quantity and store it, soften it with cream, beat it up with hot chillies or enrich it with peanut butter (see below) or whatever you fancy.

2 tablespoons (30 ml) olive oil

1 small onion, peeled and very finely chopped

1 clove garlic, peeled and finely chopped

1 × 14 oz (400 g) can of plum tomatoes, drained and roughly chopped

1 teaspoon dried basil

salt and pepper to taste

Heat the oil in a medium saucepan over a low heat, add the onion and the garlic and cook carefully for 5–7 minutes until the onion is soft but not browned. Stir in the chopped plum tomatoes, add the basil, and cook, covered, for 15–20 minutes. Inspect the sauce during this period and stir if necessary. Season with salt and pepper. This sauce is good hot or cold.

Peanut Sauce (*Salsa de Maní*)

Makes about ¼ pint (150 ml)

This sauce is good with potato dishes. Try it with the Potato Cakes (see page 72).

2 tablespoons (30 ml) peanut butter	½ recipe quantity Basic Tomato Sauce (see page 80)

Blend or whisk the peanut butter into the tomato sauce. Add a little tomato juice or water if the sauce is too thick to pour relatively easily.

Raw Tomato Sauce (*Salcita de Jitomate*)

Makes ½ pint (275 ml)

Use good fresh ripe tomatoes for this sauce.

1 lb (450 g) ripe tomatoes, skinned and seeded (see page 19)	2 tablespoons (30 ml) olive oil
	1 tablespoon (15 ml) finely chopped parsley
1 tablespoon (15 ml) wine vinegar	1 teaspoon dried basil
	salt and black pepper to taste

Place all the ingredients in a blender or food processor and process until a smooth sauce is obtained.

Béchamel Sauce (*Salsa Blanca*)

Makes about 14 fl oz (400 ml)

1 oz (25 g) butter	½ pint (275 ml) milk
2 tablespoons (30 ml) finely diced onion	bay leaf
	pinch of nutmeg
1 oz (25 g) wholemeal flour	salt and black pepper to taste

Melt the butter in a heavy saucepan over a low heat. Add the onion and sauté until softened and transparent. Stir in the flour to form a smooth paste and cook, stirring, for 2–3 minutes. Add the milk to the pan slowly, stirring constantly. Continue cooking and stirring until the sauce thickens. Add the bay leaf, nutmeg and salt and black pepper and simmer, covered, over a very low heat for 10 minutes. Stir occasionally.

Cheese Sauce (*Salsa de Queso*)

Makes about ¾ pint (450 ml)

2 oz (50 g) Cheddar or
    Gruyère cheese, grated
1 recipe quantity Béchamel
    Sauce (see page 80)

1 teaspoon prepared English
    mustard (optional)

Stir the grated cheese into the cooked béchamel sauce until it has melted. For extra flavour, stir in the mustard if you wish.

Mustard Sauce (*Salsa de Mostaza*)

Makes 6 fl oz (175 ml)

Serve over cooked vegetables.

3 tablespoons (45 ml)
    prepared mustard of your
    choice
4 fl oz (100 ml) olive oil
1 tablespoon (15 ml) red wine
    vinegar

salt to taste
2 tablespoons (30 ml) finely
    chopped fresh parsley

Put the mustard in a small bowl and slowly beat in the oil and vinegar, adding a little of each at a time. When well blended, carefully add salt to taste. Stir in the parsley and serve.

Avocado Sauce (*Salsa de Aguacate*)

Makes ½ pint (275 ml)

This cold sauce is good with cooked vegetables or as a dip for raw vegetables, bread and tortillas etc.

1 large ripe avocado
1 tablespoon (15 ml) lime
    juice
¼ pint (150 ml) soured cream,
    crème fraîche or thick plain
    yoghurt

2 tablespoons (30 ml) finely
    chopped fresh coriander
salt and chilli sauce (optional)
    to taste

Halve the avocado, remove the stone and scoop out the flesh. Beat into a cream with the other ingredients, either by hand or using a blender or food processor. Serve immediately.

SALAD DRESSINGS

Basic Vinaigrette Dressing

Makes 6 fl oz (175 ml)

¼ pint (150 ml) vegetable oil
2 tablespoons (30 ml) wine
    vinegar, cider vinegar or
    lemon juice

salt and pepper to taste
1 teaspoon prepared mustard
    (optional)

Place all the ingredients in a bowl or blender and beat or blend well. Test and adjust seasoning if necessary.

Basic Mayonnaise

Makes about ½ pint (275 ml)

1 large egg
1 teaspoon prepared mustard
good pinch of salt
9 fl oz (250 ml) vegetable oil
lemon juice or wine vinegar
    (up to 2 tablespoons (30 ml)
    to taste)

additional salt, black pepper,
    paprika or cayenne pepper
    to taste

Break the egg into a bowl or blender goblet and add the mustard and pinch of salt. Beat or blend at medium speed until the mixture thickens slightly. Still beating or blending, pour in the oil from a measuring jug, drop by drop initially and then, as it begins to thicken, in a slow but steady stream until all the oil is absorbed. Carefully beat or blend in the lemon juice or wine vinegar and season to taste with additional salt, pepper, paprika or cayenne pepper. Store in a cool place. Mayonnaise will keep for not much longer than a day.

Guacamole   MEXICO

Serves 4–6 as a starter

This Mexican spiced creamy avocado sauce/dressing may be served with almost any savoury dish, but it is especially used as a spread on tortillas, as a dip or sauce for raw or parboiled vegetables and for serving as a starter with tortilla chips or bread. Two ingredients lists are given here. Ingredients 1 gives a very tasty but milder version, more to the European taste. Ingredients 2 gives a hotter, simpler, more South American version. Remember, Mexicans consider avocados to be an aphrodisiac!

INGREDIENTS 1

2 large ripe avocados
1 large beefsteak tomato or 2 large ordinary tomatoes, skinned, seeded (see page 19), juiced and chopped
2 tablespoons (30 ml) finely chopped onion
1 tablespoon (15 ml) chopped fresh coriander leaves

1 tablespoon (15 ml) lemon or lime juice
1 clove garlic, peeled and very finely chopped
1 fresh chilli pepper, seeded and very finely chopped or hot pepper sauce to taste
1 teaspoon paprika (optional)
salt and pepper to taste

INGREDIENTS 2

2 large ripe avocados
2 fresh green chilli peppers, seeded and finely chopped
1 tablespoon (15 ml) chopped fresh coriander leaves
2 tablespoons (30 ml) finely chopped onion

1 large beefsteak tomato or 2 large ordinary tomatoes, skinned (see page 19)
salt to taste

Peel and halve the avocados, remove the stones and dice the flesh. Place in a steep-sided mixing bowl. Add all the other ingredients and mix well, but not so well that all trace of the separate ingredients disappears. Serve immediately.

Note: Guacamole deteriorates quickly once it has been made, because avocado blackens in contact with the air. If you have any left over, you can extend its life by almost filling a small container with it and then sealing the top with a thin layer of vegetable oil. When you want to serve the guacamole, pour off the excess oil and stir in any that remains on the surface.

Avocado Dressing

Makes about ½ pint (275 ml)

This thick, spicy, hot dressing is good with chopped raw vegetables, such as carrots, young cauliflower, celery and tender courgettes. For a thinner less filling dressing, omit the hard-boiled egg.

1 ripe avocado
1 hard-boiled egg, shelled
4 fl oz (100 ml) olive oil
3 tablespoons (45 ml) white
   wine vinegar
1 tablespoon (15 ml) tomato
   purée
½–1 teaspoon hot pepper sauce
salt to taste

Halve the avocado, remove the stone and scoop the flesh into a blender or food processor. Add the remaining ingredients and blend until the dressing is smooth.

Note: For a milder or hotter dressing, adjust the amount of hot pepper sauce used.

Tortillas, Tortilla Dishes and Breads

The recipes given in this chapter are not specific to one country, although the names we have used for tortillas and their products are Mexican in origin.

TORTILLAS
Tortillas, flat breads made from corn and/or wheat dough, are an indispensable part of Latin American eating. Apart from the basic soft-textured variety, they are also processed into many other shapes and textures (see Tortilla Dishes on pages 88–94). The Spanish conquistadores, faced with a litany of Aztec names for tortillas and their products, simply called them tortillas after the similarly shaped potato omelette which was common in their own country.

The traditional way to make tortillas is from fresh or dried corn kernels, soaked in lime, then boiled, rinsed, drained and pressed into a dough (*masa*). This dough is either pressed or rolled and shaped to make the tortillas or it is dried and ground into a flour (*masa harina*) which is then used to make the tortilla dough. The tortillas are cooked on a stone griddle over a fire. The following extract from *The Book of Whole Grains* by Marlene Ann Bumgarner describes this process:

> Begin with 2 pounds of corn kernals, 2 ounces of powdered lime
> (available from hardware stores) and 3 quarts of water.
>
> Wash the corn, add lime and water, and boil until the kernal skins
> loosen. Remove from heat and cool. Rub handfuls of the kernals
> between the palms of your hands until the skins are loosened and
> removed. Wash kernals thoroughly in cold water to remove lime.
> You now have *nixtamal* – grind it in a food mill, meat grinder, or
> large mortar and pestle into a soft dough. Divide into small balls
> and work each into round flat disks about 7 inches in diameter and
> very thin.
>
> In Mexico tortillas are baked on a *comal*, an ungreased clay or iron
> baking griddle, over a flame. Any griddle or large heavy skillet will
> work well, however. Bake on one side until tinged with brown and
> fragrant, then turn and bake on other side. Keep warm in a basket
> covered with a cloth. Serve hot.

Wheat and mixed corn and wheat tortillas are also popular in parts
of South and Central America, especially in North Mexico.

You can buy fresh and frozen ready-made tortillas in specialist food
shops and even in some supermarkets, but it is fun to make your
own and below we have given recipes for both corn and wheat tortillas. The first uses *masa harina*, which is fairly widely available in
the USA, but usually only obtainable from specialist suppliers (see
page 137) in Britain. The cornmeal (or whole maize flour) used in
the second recipe is readily available from wholefood and health
food shops. Don't worry if the first tortillas you make are not perfect. Like making pancakes, it takes a few tries before you get into
the swing of it.

Corn Tortillas (*Tortillas de Maíz*)

Makes 12

8 oz (225 g) masa harina
1 teaspoon salt

about 8 fl oz (225 ml) very hot
water

Stir the masa harina and salt together in a bowl and gradually add the water, stirring rapidly, to form a fairly stiff dough (it should not stick to your hands or the sides of the bowl). Work the dough gently with your hands for a few minutes, then form it into 12 balls. Place a ball of dough between two sheets of greaseproof paper and gently roll it out to form a circle about 6 in (15 cm) in diameter (this requires a light touch and Mexican cooks use a rolling pin more akin to a length of broom handle than to the heavier type we normally use). Repeat this rolling out process with the remaining balls of dough.

Heat a very slightly greased heavy frying pan over a moderate heat and cook each tortilla for 1–2 minutes on each side until dry and slightly puffed up with dark patches. The pan should sizzle slightly as you put the tortillas in, if it is the right temperature. The tortillas should be supple and bendy rather than hard, so it is best to under-cook rather than overcook them. As each tortilla comes out of the pan, place it in a towel- or cloth-lined basket and wrap to keep warm while you cook the rest.

Tortillas will keep for 4–5 days wrapped in a towel inside a plastic bag in the refrigerator. They will also freeze well. To make them soft and pliable again, heat for a few seconds on each side in an ungreased frying pan or hold them, with tongs, directly over a gas flame.

Corn and Wheat Tortillas
(*Tortillas de Harina de Maíz y Trigo*)

Makes 12

4 oz (100 g) cornmeal
  (stoneground if available)
6 fl oz (175 ml) water, boiling
1 tablespoon (15 ml) vegetable
  oil

6 oz (175 g) fine wholemeal or
  plain unbleached flour
1 teaspoon salt
1½ oz (40 g) vegetable
  margarine or shortening

Combine the cornmeal, boiling water and oil in a bowl and stir well.
Set aside for 7–8 minutes. Meanwhile, stir together the flour and salt
in a large mixing bowl and then rub in the margarine or shortening
until the mixture resembles fine crumbs. Add the cornmeal mixture
and beat it in with a wooden spoon to form a fairly stiff dough (it
should not stick to your hands or the sides of the bowl). Knead the
dough gently for a few minutes and then form it into 12 balls. Now
roll out and cook as for Corn Tortillas (see page 87).

Wheat Tortillas (*Tortillas de Harina de Trigo*)

Makes 12

8 oz (225 g) unbleached plain
  flour or 4 oz (100 g)
  unbleached plain flour and
  4 oz (100 g) fine wholemeal
  flour

1 teaspoon salt
2 oz (50 g) vegetable
  margarine or shortening
about ¼ pint (150 ml) hand
  hot water

Mix together the flour and salt in a bowl and rub in the margarine or
shortening until the mixture resembles fine crumbs. Gradually add
the water to make a fairly stiff dough (it should not stick to your
hands or the sides of the bowl). Knead the dough gently for a few
minutes, then form it into 12 balls. Now roll out and cook as for
Corn Tortillas (see page 87).

TORTILLA DISHES
Tortillas and tortilla-like doughs are the basis for a variety of other
dishes.

Tacos
Tacos are simply corn tortillas wrapped around a savoury filling.
They can be served soft or crisply fried.

Soft Tacos

To serve soft tacos, simply place one or more fillings (see pages 94–7), kept warm over a spirit burner or similar, plus garnishes (see Fried Tacos, below) on the table with a pile of fresh warm tortillas (about 2–3 per person). People can then help themselves by taking a tortilla, spooning on some filling, folding it up and then eating it.

Fried Tacos

Serves 4–6

12 Corn Tortillas (see page 87)
1 recipe quantity of filling (see pages 94–7)

2 tablespoons (30 ml) vegetable oil

GARNISH
a selection from the following:

Salsa Cruda or Salsa Fresca (see page 75), shredded lettuce, grated cheese, sliced tomatoes, chopped fresh coriander, sliced onion, sliced black olives, soured cream or crème fraîche

Heat the tortillas in an ungreased frying pan on both sides for a few seconds to soften them up. Place a couple of spoonfuls of the chosen filling down the middle of each tortilla and then fold them in half over it. Heat the vegetable oil in a heavy frying pan and fry the filled tortillas (tacos), one or two at a time, on both sides until just crisp. Drain on absorbent kitchen paper and serve hot with a selection of the garnishes. The garnishes may be pushed into the tacos. Guacamole is also a traditional accompaniment to tacos.

Alternatively, you can make taco shells by shallow-frying the flat tortillas for a couple of minutes on each side, then, as soon as they are cooked, hanging them over a rolling pin or something similar and leaving to cool. They will set into shape and become crisp. Fill with the savoury filling and top with garnishes. Or just leave the fried tortillas flat and top, open faced, with some filling and garnishes.

To eat, just pick the whole thing up and bite into it. It tends to break into pieces with the filling or topping falling on to your lap, but that's the way they do it in South America!

Note: You can, if you wish, use shop-bought taco shells. Just prepare the filling, stuff it into the shells and serve with the garnishes.

Burritos

Burritos are essentially tacos made with large wheat tortillas. Use the Wheat Tortillas recipe on page 88 and roll out the dough to make six 10 in (25.5 cm) tortillas, then proceed as for Soft or Fried Tacos (see page 89).

Tostadas

Tostadas are tortillas baked crisp in the oven and served, open faced, with a savoury topping and salad garnishes. They are almost identical to open faced fried tacos. To prepare, brush the tortillas with a little oil, season with salt and black pepper and bake in the oven at 225°F (110°C, gas mark ¼) for 1 hour. Remove, spread with one of the fillings given on pages 94–7 and top with a selection of the garnishes suggested for Fried Tacos (see page 89).

Tostaditas

Tostaditas or tortilla chips are wedges or strips of tortilla fried until crisp. Serve with a bowl of Salsa Cruda or Salsa Fresca (see page 75). They may also be arranged in an ovenproof dish, topped with cheese and refried beans (see page 107) and baked in the oven at 350°F (180°C, gas mark 4) for about 10 minutes or until warmed through and the cheese has melted. Again, serve with Salsa Cruda or Salsa Fresca.

Chilaquiles

This is a casserole made by frying stale tortillas until crisp and then layering them with cheese and vegetables and pouring over a chilli-based sauce (see pages 75–9) or stock.

Enchiladas

Enchiladas are corn tortillas that have been dipped in a savoury sauce, then sometimes in hot oil, before being rolled up, often around a savoury filling, and baked, usually in more of the savoury sauce. The fillings given in the following recipes can be replaced by any of fillings given on pages 94–7.

Enchiladas with Mushroom Filling in Hot Sauce
(Enchiladas Rellenas con Chamañones y Salsa Picante)

Serves 6

Serve with a dressed green salad.

1 large tomato	12 Corn Tortillas (see page 87)
1 clove garlic	
1 small onion	1 lb (450 g) mushrooms, wiped, thinly sliced and cooked until soft in a little oil
1 small green bell pepper	
1–2 fresh green chilli peppers	
salt and pepper to taste	
2 tablespoons (30 ml) vegetable oil	3 oz (75 g) Cheddar cheese, grated
about 8 fl oz (225 ml) vegetable stock or water	1 tablespoon (15 ml) finely chopped onion

Put the tomato, garlic clove, onion, bell pepper and chilli peppers on a grill pan and place under a hot grill until the skin of the bell pepper just starts to bubble. Remove the skin from the garlic clove and onion and skin and deseed the bell pepper. Place all of them in a blender or food processor and process until smooth. Add salt and pepper to taste. Heat the oil in a large frying pan and fry this sauce until reduced and thick, then add enough stock or water to make a light coating consistency. Set aside.

Preheat the oven to 350°F (180°C, gas mark 4). Soften the tortillas by heating them very briefly on both sides in an ungreased frying pan or holding them, in tongs, over a gas flame. Dip them in the sauce, turning and coating each one well. Place a portion of the mushrooms on each, roll up and place, seam side down, in a buttered ovenproof dish in one layer. Spoon over any remaining sauce, sprinkle with the cheese and bake for 30 minutes in the hot oven. Garnish with the chopped onion and serve.

Note: An alternative and less difficult method of handling the tortillas is to spread about 2 tablespoons (30 ml) of the sauce over one side of each of them, then fill, roll up and bake as directed above. Towards the end of the baking time, reheat any leftover sauce and just before serving, pour it over the enchiladas.

Enchiladas with Cheese Filling
(*Enchiladas Rellenas con Queso*)

Serves 4

This is a simplified quick version of the traditional method of preparing enchiladas.

4 tablespoons (60 ml) vegetable oil or melted butter

1 medium onion, peeled and finely diced

1 lb (450 g) Cheddar cheese, grated

2 tablespoons (30 ml) finely chopped parsley

1 fresh green chilli pepper, seeded and chopped or ½ teaspoon chilli powder

¼ teaspoon ground cumin

salt and black pepper to taste

8 Corn Tortillas (see page 87)

1 recipe quantity Basic Tomato Sauce (see page 79)

Preheat the oven to 375°F (190°C, gas mark 5). Heat half the oil or butter in a frying pan and sauté the onion until softened. Combine the cheese, parsley, chilli pepper or chilli powder, cumin and seasoning with the onion and the oil it was cooked in. Mix this filling well and set aside. Soften the tortillas by heating them very briefly on both sides in an ungreased frying pan or holding them, in tongs, over a gas flame. Put a portion of the cheese filling down the middle of each tortilla and roll up. Place the stuffed tortillas on a greased baking dish, seam side down, and brush the tops with the remaining oil or butter. Now cover them with tomato sauce and bake in the preheated oven for 25 minutes. Serve.

Variations Replace part or all of the cheese with the same weight of cooked red kidney beans. Alternatively, kidney beans can be combined with cooked vegetables and/or rice.

Quesadillas

Quesadillas are uncooked corn tortillas that have been folded over a savoury filling and then either deep-fried or baked in a hot oven until crisp and golden. To prepare enough for 4–6 people, follow the Corn Tortillas recipe on page 87, but leave the tortillas uncooked. Then prepare one of the savoury fillings given on pages 94–7 (or simply use grated cheese). Place a portion of filling on one half of each uncooked tortilla, then fold the other half over the filling and pinch the edges together to seal. Then either brush the filled tortillas with oil and bake in a preheated oven at 400°F (200°C, gas mark 6) for about 15–20 minutes or deep-fry in hot oil until crisp and golden.

Chimichangas

Chimichangas are the same as quesadillas, except they are made using uncooked wheat tortillas (see page 88).

Tamales

Tamales are made with a tortilla-like dough prepared from *masa* or *masa harina*, fat and sometimes baking powder. This is wrapped around a savoury or sweet filling, such as whole or mashed beans, cooked vegetables, fruit or nuts. The uncooked tamales are then wrapped in corn husks or banana leaves and steamed. Tamales come in every shape and size, from tiny one-bite nibbles to large plump parcels.

Empanadas

These are savoury pastries made by wrapping a white flour dough around a savoury filling and baking. Sometimes the dough is enriched with spices or cheese (try experimenting with the recipe given below). They are very popular all over Latin America.

Empanadas

Makes about 16

10 oz (275 g) unbleached plain flour or 6 oz (175 g) unbleached plain flour and 4 oz (100 g) cornmeal or masa harina
1 teaspoon baking powder
pinch of salt

4 oz vegetable margarine or shortening
1 egg, beaten
4 fl oz (100 ml) milk
1 recipe quantity of filling (see pages 94–7)

Sift together the flour or flours, baking powder and salt into a large bowl. Rub in the vegetable margarine or shortening until the mixture resembles fine crumbs. Beat together the egg and milk and stir into the flour mixture to form a firm smooth dough. Knead the dough for a few seconds, then form into a ball. Cover this with a cloth and set aside in the refrigerator for 15–30 minutes.

Preheat the oven to 350°F (180°C, gas mark 4). On a floured surface, roll out the prepared dough to about ⅛ in (3 mm) thick. Cut the dough into 5 in (12.5 cm) diameter circles. Knead and reroll scraps of dough for additional circles. Place 2–3 tablespoons (30–45 ml) filling on each circle, brush the edges with a little milk, fold over and press the edges together to seal with the tines of a fork.

Place on a lightly greased baking sheet and bake in the preheated oven for 20 minutes or until golden brown.

Variation Instead of preparing the dough as above, simply use 1 lb (450 g) puff pastry, bought ready-made (chilled or frozen).

SAVOURY FILLINGS
Guacamole (see page 83) and refried beans (see page 107) are both traditional fillings for tacos, burritos, tostadas, enchiladas, quesadillas, empanadas etc. You could also try some of the fillings given below and experimenting with your own ideas.

Avocado and Cheese (*Aguacate y Queso*)

For 12 tacos, enchiladas, tostadas etc.

3 medium ripe avocados
1 clove garlic, peeled and
  finely chopped
1 small onion, peeled and
  finely diced
¼ teaspoon hot pepper sauce

½ teaspoon ground cumin
juice of ½ lemon
salt and black pepper to taste
6 oz (175 g) Cheddar cheese,
  grated

Halve the avocados, remove the stones and scoop out the flesh into a bowl. Combine with all the other ingredients except the cheese. Mash well together. Adjust the seasoning, stir in the cheese and use.

Potato and Egg (*Papa y Huevo*)

For 12 tacos, enchiladas, tostadas etc.

2 tablespoons (30 ml)
  vegetable oil
1 small onion, peeled and
  finely chopped

1 lb (450 g) potatoes, peeled,
  cooked and diced
3 eggs, beaten
salt and black pepper to taste

Heat the oil in a pan and sauté the onion until softened. Add the potatoes and sauté until the potatoes are gently browned. Pour in the beaten eggs, season to taste with salt and black pepper and cook, stirring, until the eggs are set.

Red Beans in Tomato Sauce
(*Frijoles Rojas en Salsa de Jitomate*)

For 12 tacos, enchiladas, tostadas etc.

2 tablespoons (30 ml)
vegetable oil
1 medium onion, peeled and
finely chopped
1 green bell pepper, seeded
and chopped
1–2 fresh or dried red or green
chilli peppers, seeded and
finely chopped
1 clove garlic, peeled and
crushed

1 lb (450 g) cooked red kidney
beans (use tinned beans or
soak 6 oz (175 g) dried
beans overnight, drain, cover
with fresh water and cook
until tender – see page 12)
6 fl oz (175 ml) Basic Tomato
Sauce (see page 79)
½ teaspoon ground cumin
salt and black pepper to taste

Heat the oil in a saucepan and sauté the onion, bell pepper, chilli
pepper and garlic until the onion is well softened. Add the beans,
tomato sauce, cumin and seasoning. Cover and simmer for 10 minutes, then use.

Fried Beans and Cheese
(*Frijoles Fritos y Queso*)

For 12 tacos, enchiladas, tostadas etc.

1 lb (450 g) cooked kidney,
pinto or brown beans (use
tinned beans or soak 6 oz
(175 g) dried beans
overnight, drain, cover with
fresh water and cook until
tender – see page 12)

4 fl oz (100 ml) bean cooking
water or juices from the tin
1 tablespoon (15 ml) vegetable
oil
salt and black pepper to taste
6 oz (175 g) Cheddar cheese,
grated

Purée the beans with the cooking water in a blender or mash by
hand. Heat the oil in a heavy pan and fry the purée, stirring constantly, until thick and creamy. Season and stir in the cheese. Continue cooking until the cheese melts, then use.

Creamy Chilli and Pepper
(*Chiles con Crema y Pimiento Negra*)

For 12 tacos, enchiladas, tostadas etc.

1 tablespoon (15 ml) vegetable
   oil
1 medium onion, peeled and
   finely sliced
4 medium green bell peppers,
   skinned (see page 13),
   seeded and cut into strips

2 fresh green chilli peppers,
   seeded and cut into narrow
   strips
salt and black pepper to taste
8 fl oz (225 ml) double cream
4 oz (100 g) Cheddar cheese,
   grated

Heat the oil in a large heavy saucepan or frying pan and sauté the onion until softened. Add the bell pepper and chilli pepper strips and seasoning, stir well and cook gently, covered, until the pepper is well softened. Stir in the cream and cheese and cook over a low heat until the cheese melts, then use.

Lentils (*Lentejas*)

For 12 tacos, enchiladas, tostadas etc.

2 tablespoons (30 ml)
   vegetable oil
1 medium onion, peeled and
   finely chopped
2 cloves garlic, peeled and
   crushed
1 fresh or dried red or green
   chilli pepper, seeded and
   finely chopped
1 lb (450 g) cooked green or
   brown lentils (use tinned
   lentils or put 6 oz (175 g)
   lentils and 2½ pints (1.5
   litres) cold water in a pan,
   bring to the boil, cover, and
   simmer for 1–1½ hours or
   until tender)

4 fl oz (100 ml) lentil cooking
   water or juice from the tin
4 tablespoons (60 ml) tomato
   purée
4 oz (100 g) sultanas
½ teaspoon paprika
juice of 1 lemon
salt and black pepper to taste

Heat the oil in a pan and sauté the onion, garlic and chilli pepper until softened. Add the drained cooked lentils, cooking water, tomato purée and sultanas. Stir well and simmer for 5 minutes. Add the paprika and lemon juice and season to taste. Stir well and simmer, covered, for a further 2–3 minutes, then use.

Mushrooms (*Chamañones*)

For 12 tacos, enchiladas, tostadas etc.

1 tablespoon (15 ml) vegetable oil
1 medium onion, peeled and finely chopped
2 cloves garlic, peeled and crushed
1 lb (450 g) mushrooms, wiped and thinly sliced
12 oz (350 g) tinned tomatoes, drained and chopped

1–2 fresh or dried red or green chilli peppers, seeded and chopped
2 tablespoons (30 ml) finely chopped fresh coriander
½ teaspoon ground cumin
salt and black pepper to taste
4 oz (100 g) Cheddar cheese, grated

Heat the oil in a heavy saucepan or frying pan and sauté the onion and garlic until softened. Add the mushrooms and sauté further until they are softened. Add the tomatoes and chilli peppers, stir, cover and simmer gently for 10 minutes. Stir in the remaining ingredients, remove from the heat and use.

BREADS

Sunflower Seed and Honey Bread

Makes a 2 lb (900 g) loaf

This is an unyeasted Indian wheat bread.

8 oz (225 g) sunflower seeds
6 oz (175 g) wholemeal flour (stoneground if available)
1 teaspoon baking powder
1 teaspoon salt

2 eggs
2 oz (50 g) butter
3 fl oz (75 ml) clear honey
8 fl oz (225 ml) milk

Preheat the oven to 350°F (180°C, gas mark 4). Using a coffee grinder or pestle and mortar, grind half the sunflower seeds into a coarse flour. Combine this with the wholemeal flour, baking powder and salt. Mix well together. Beat the eggs, butter, honey and milk well together and then stir this mixture into the flour mix. Add the remaining sunflower seeds and knead into a smooth dough. Transfer to a greased 2 lb (900 g) bread tin and bake in the preheated oven for 1 hour or until a fine skewer inserted into the middle comes out clean. Remove from the oven and leave to cool before removing from the tin.

Yeasted Cornbread (*Pao de Milho*)   BRAZIL

Makes 2 × 1 lb (450 g) loaves

Cornbread is a delicious alternative to regular bread, although it is much richer and is usually served in smaller portions. Try it particularly with bean dishes or even on its own with a cheese and/or tomato sauce.

2 oz (50 g) butter
8 fl oz (225 ml) hot milk
4 fl oz (100 ml) water
1 tablespoon (15 ml) sugar
1 teaspoon salt
1 × ¼ oz (7 g) sachet active
    dried yeast

12 oz (350 g) unbleached plain
    flour, plus a little extra as
    needed
8 oz (225 g) cornmeal
    (stoneground if available)
2 eggs

Combine in a large mixing bowl the butter, milk, water, sugar and salt and stir well to dissolve the solids. Stir in the yeast and set aside. Sift together the plain flour and cornmeal. Add the eggs to the yeast mixture and beat well. Then beat in the plain flour and cornmeal and enough of the extra flour to form a pliable but not sticky dough. Cover and set aside in a warm place for 2 hours (it should be well risen and have almost doubled in size). Knead the dough and divide it into two halves. Press each half of dough into a greased 1 lb (450 g) bread tin and set aside, covered, for 30 minutes to rise again. Near the end of this time, preheat the oven to 375°F (190°C, gas mark 5). Bake in the oven for 45 minutes or until the top is browned and a fine skewer inserted in the middle of a loaf comes out clean.

Unyeasted Cornbread
(*Pan de Harina de Maíz*)

Makes approximately a 2 lb (900 g) loaf or 8–10 muffins

2 eggs
¾ pint (450 ml) buttermilk or
   8 fl oz (225 ml) natural low-
   fat yoghurt and 8 fl oz
   (225 ml) milk
1 teaspoon baking powder

8 oz (225 g) cornmeal
   (stoneground if available)
1 teaspoon salt
1–2 fresh chilli peppers, seeded
   and finely chopped
   (optional)

Preheat the oven to 400°F (200°C, gas mark 6). Grease a 9 in (23 cm) square (or similar area) cake tin and place it in the oven to preheat. Combine all the ingredients and beat them well together. Pour into the prepared tin and bake in the oven for 25–30 minutes or until a skewer inserted into the middle comes out clean. Cool slightly, turn out of the tin, cut into wedges and serve with butter. Alternatively, divide the mixture between 8–10 greased muffin tins and bake for about 15–20 minutes.

Variations Add 4 oz (100 g) grated Cheddar cheese to the mixture and sprinkle a little extra on top before baking. This variation is particularly good if you also include the chilli peppers.

For a sweet version, replace half the cornmeal with wholemeal flour and the chilli pepper with 2 tablespoons (30 ml) honey.

Bean and Rice Dishes

Beans and rice, properly prepared, are excellent and versatile staple foods. Served either as accompaniments to a main dish or as one of the ingredients, they combine well, separately and together, with many other foods. Beans and rice eaten together at the same meal complement one another's protein content, providing a rich source of 'complete' protein.

BEANS

Beans are indigenous to South America and they have been found in Peruvian graves dating back to 3800 BC. Beans are part of the great South American culinary trio, which also includes corn (maize) and squash. To peasant farmers the cultivation of beans is most important, since, unlike corn and squash, they help make the soil nitrogen-rich, so that after they have been harvested, it is then possible to grow healthy corn and squash in the same plot. Beans, along with corn, are still the most widely eaten food in Latin America and they are an intrinsic part of most peoples' diet.

In Mexico in particular there are many varieties of bean to choose from and in any Mexican food market there will be pile upon pile of beans, for example the shiny beetle-like *frijoles negros*, the delicate yellow-pink shades of *canarios*, the brown-speckled *ojo de cabra* or 'goats' eyes' beans and the huge multi-coloured *ayocotes*. Beans are generally cooked and presented in a soupy sauce, traditionally in bowls, after the main course and before the sweet course at the main meal of the day. They may also be mashed and fried in oil to make a smooth paste called *frijoles refritos* (refried beans – see page 107). They are often used in this way in tortilla dishes.

In Brazilian cookery, which has strong African and American Indian influences, black beans, cassava meal and rice are the three basic culinary ingredients, although the bean is king of the trio. The black bean or *feijao preto* is the hallmark of Brazilian cooking, although others, such as black-eyed peas and red, white and pink beans, turn up in many dishes.

Venezuelans also enjoy black beans. They call their *caraotas negras* (a popular bean dish – see page 102) *'caviar Criollo'* (Creole caviar) and serve it as an hors d'œuvre.

For instructions on preparing and cooking all types of dried beans, see page 12.

Bean and Banana Dip   ECUADOR
(*Entremés de Banana y Frijoles*)

Serves 4–6

As well as being a dip, this dish, served with a big green salad, would also be more than adequate as the main course of a simple meal.

2 tablespoons (30 ml) olive oil
1 onion, peeled and finely chopped
2 cloves garlic, peeled and crushed
3 red bell peppers, seeded and chopped into large chunks
2 small green chilli peppers, seeded and finely chopped
1 × 14 oz (400 g) can of tomatoes, roughly chopped

1 lb (450 g) cooked kidney beans (use tinned beans or soak 6 oz (175 g) dried beans overnight, drain, cover with fresh water and cook until tender – see page 12)
4 ripe but still firm bananas, peeled and thickly sliced

Heat the oil in a pan and fry the onion until soft and transparent. Add the garlic and sauté for a further 1–2 minutes. Add the chunks of bell pepper, the chilli peppers and the tomatoes. Cook together for 10 minutes over a moderate heat. Mash half of the beans with a potato masher. Add these with the remaining whole beans to the vegetable mixture. Cover and cook over a low heat for 5 minutes. Add the bananas, and cook for a further 5 minutes. Serve warm in bowls.

Caviar Black Beans   VENEZUELA
(*Caraotas Negras*)

Serves 4–6 as a starter

Whatever their social or economic position, Venezuelans love beans. This is one dish, made from black beans, that is particularly popular.

8 oz (225 g) dried black beans,
   soaked overnight in cold
   water
1 large onion, peeled and
   roughly chopped
¼ pint (150 ml) olive oil

3 cloves garlic, peeled and
   crushed
2 dried red chilli peppers,
   seeded and chopped
2 teaspoons cumin seeds
salt to taste

Drain and rinse the beans, cover with fresh water in a large pan, bring to the boil, boil vigorously for 10 minutes, lower the heat and leave to simmer for 1 hour or until tender. Drain them and set aside. Sauté the onion in 2 tablespoons (30 ml) of the olive oil until it is soft. Add the garlic, chilli peppers and the cumin seeds. Cook for a further 5 minutes. Add the drained beans and the rest of the olive oil. Season to taste with salt. Mix well and serve at room temperature.

Bean and Vegetable Stew (*Porotos Granados*)

CHILE

Serves 4–6

This generous stew is the national dish of Chile, but is common all over South America. It has a decidedly American Indian flavour, with tomatoes, beans, corn and marrow as its major ingredients.

8 oz (225 g) dried haricot
   beans, soaked overnight in
   cold water
3 tablespoons (45 ml) olive oil
2 medium onions, peeled and
   finely chopped
2 cloves garlic, peeled and
   crushed
2 tablespoons (30 ml) mild
   paprika
2 dried red chilli peppers,
   seeded and finely chopped
8 oz (225 g) frozen or tinned
   sweetcorn

1 lb (450 g) pumpkin, marrow
   or other squash, cut in 1 in
   (2.5 cm) cubes
1 lb (450 g) fresh tomatoes,
   skinned, seeded (see page
   19) and roughly chopped or
   1 × 14 oz (400 g) can of
   chopped tomatoes
½ teaspoon dried thyme
½ teaspoon dried basil
salt and ground black pepper
   to taste

Drain and rinse the beans, cover with fresh water in a large pan, bring to the boil, boil vigorously for 10 minutes, lower the heat and leave to simmer for 1–1½ hours or until tender. Drain and set aside, reserving about half of the bean liquid. Heat the oil in a large saucepan. Add the onions and fry until soft. Stir in the garlic and paprika and fry for a further 5 minutes. Add all the remaining ingredients and simmer for 15 minutes to blend the flavours. Add some bean liquid if the mixture becomes too dry. Simmer until the marrow or squash has disintegrated. Serve hot in large bowls with rice and/or tortillas and *pebre* sauce (see below).

Pebre

Traditionally served with Chile's national dish, *porotos granados* (see above), this simple chilli-hot coriander sauce could easily accompany other dishes.

2 tablespoons (30 ml) corn oil
1 tablespoon (15 ml) lemon
  juice
¼ pint (150 ml) water
2 oz (50 g) fresh coriander
  leaves, chopped

1 clove garlic, peeled and
  crushed
½ teaspoon salt
4–6 hot red chilli peppers,
  seeded and finely chopped

Combine the oil, lemon juice and water with a balloon whisk. Stir in the remaining ingredients and mix well. Allow the sauce to stand at room temperature for at least 3 hours. Correct the seasoning and serve.

Chickpeas with Spinach   BRAZIL
(*Grao com Espinafres*)

Serves 4

An unusual but very tasty combination, this is generally served as a side dish, but it is also good on its own as a light lunch dish, served with tortillas.

8 oz (225 g) dried chickpeas,
  soaked overnight
2 lb (900 g) fresh spinach
2 medium onions, peeled and
  sliced

salt and black pepper to taste
¼ pint (150 ml) vegetable
  stock
3 tablespoons (45 ml) olive oil

Drain and rinse the chickpeas. Wash the spinach well. Put the spinach and chickpeas in a large saucepan in layers with the sliced onion. Season each layer. Add the vegetable stock and dribble the olive oil over the vegetables. Cover the saucepan and cook over a very low heat for 2–2½ hours, or until the chickpeas are tender. Add a little water if the mixture becomes too dry during cooking, but note that when the dish is cooked, all the liquid should have been absorbed.

Lentils with Fruit and Sweet Potatoes (*Lentejas con Fruta y Camote*)

Serves 8

This quick-to-make casserole dish is an exotic and unusual combination of ingredients and flavours. It improves with standing and it is worth making enough for two meals.

1 lb (450 g) green or brown lentils, soaked for 4 hours or overnight

1 tablespoon (15 ml) vegetable oil

1 small onion, peeled and diced

1 clove garlic, peeled and crushed

1 × 14 oz (400 g) can of plum tomatoes, puréed

8 oz (225 g) fresh or tinned pineapple chunks

2 firm pears, peeled, cored and chopped

1 large sweet potato, washed (scrubbed if dirty), sliced and parboiled

1 plantain or large green banana, peeled and sliced

salt and black pepper to taste

Drain the lentils, put in a large pan and cover with cold water. Bring to the boil, reduce the heat and simmer, covered, for about 40–45 minutes, until almost tender. Meanwhile, heat the oil in a frying pan and sauté the onion and garlic until soft. Add the puréed tomatoes and cook over a low heat for 5 minutes. Add this mixture to the almost cooked lentils along with the remaining ingredients. Cook over a moderate heat until the pears and banana are almost tender.

Haricot Beans in Olive Sauce
(*Habas en Salsa de Aceittunas*)

PERU

Serves 4

This dish would traditionally have been made with Lima beans, said to be the aristocrat of beans. As they are not easy to obtain here, we have substituted haricot beans, a good replacement. Use the best olives you can afford (Kalamata olives from Greece, for example).

1 lb (450 g) dried Lima or haricot beans, soaked overnight
2 dried red chilli peppers, seeded and crumbled
½ in (1.2 cm) piece of ginger root, peeled and chopped
8 oz (225 g) black olives, pitted

2 tablespoons (30 ml) olive oil
2 large cloves garlic, peeled and crushed
6 spring onions, trimmed and shredded
1 stick celery, trimmed and thinly sliced

Drain and rinse the beans. Cover them with fresh cold water, bring to the boil, boil vigorously for 10 minutes, lower the heat and leave to simmer for 1–1½ hours or until tender. Drain and set aside to cool. Take about a third of the beans, mash them with a potato masher and set aside. Place the crumbled chilli peppers and the chopped ginger in ¼ pint (150 ml) of very hot water. Leave to infuse for 15 minutes, then process in a blender until smooth. Set aside. Next put the pitted olives and another ¼ pint (150 ml) of hot water in the blender and purée until smooth. Set aside. Heat the olive oil in a saucepan. Stir in the garlic and fry gently. Add the chilli and ginger mixture and cook for 10 minutes, stirring until most of the liquid has been driven off. Add the puréed olives and cook, stirring for 3 minutes. Next stir in the mashed beans, turn down the heat and continue cooking for another 5 minutes. Add the whole beans and cook for 15 minutes, stirring gently from time to time. Remove from the heat. Serve hot with the shredded spring onions and sliced celery sprinkled over.

Pickled Black Beans
(*Frijoles Negros Escabechados*)

PERU

Serves 4–6

Peruvians serve this tasty dish with rice, but it is just as good served as a salad on top of a bed of shredded lettuce leaves, garnished with hard-boiled eggs. It is at its best served at room temperature.

6 oz (175 g) dried black beans, soaked overnight in cold water

2 large onions, peeled and thickly sliced

salt

¼ pint (150 ml) red wine vinegar

3 tablespoons (45 ml) corn oil

4 oz (100 g) dried raisins

3 cloves garlic, peeled and crushed

2 teaspoons cumin seeds

2 dried red chilli peppers, seeded and crumbled

black pepper to taste

4 oz (100 g) black olives, pitted

2 hard-boiled eggs, shelled and roughly chopped

Drain and rinse the beans. Cover them in fresh water, bring to the boil, boil vigorously for 10 minutes, lower the heat and leave to simmer for 1 hour or until tender. Drain and set aside. While the beans are cooking, boil the onion slices in salted water for 3 minutes. Drain them and mix them with the wine vinegar in a bowl. Set aside. Heat the oil in a large saucepan. Add the raisins, garlic, cumin seeds and crumbled chilli peppers. Cook for 5 minutes. Add the beans, the onion and some of the red wine vinegar (enough to keep the dish moist). Stir well and simmer for 10 minutes. Season and serve, garnished with the black olives and the hard-boiled eggs.

Refried Beans (*Frijoles Refritos*)

MEXICO

Serves 4

The larger Mexican red bean is ideal for this dish, but pinto, black and kidney beans can also be used and are more readily available in Europe. When using kidney beans, make sure they are not too soft when cooked or they will not give the best result.

RECIPE 1

This makes an ideal filling for tortilla dishes (see pages 88–94).

12 oz (350 g) dried red kidney beans, soaked overnight in cold water

2 large onions, peeled and chopped

3 cloves garlic, peeled and crushed

½ teaspoon chilli powder

3 oz (75 g) butter

1 × 14 oz (400 g) can of chopped tomatoes

salt to taste

Drain the beans and rinse them under cold water. Put into a saucepan and cover with 2 pints (1.2 litres) cold water, one of the chopped onions, one of the crushed garlic cloves and the chilli powder. Bring to the boil, boil rapidly for 10 minutes, then turn down the heat and simmer gently for about 1 hour, with a lid on the saucepan. The beans should be tender but not too soft and the liquid absorbed. Melt the butter in another saucepan and fry the remaining onion and garlic in it until soft. Add the chopped tomatoes and simmer for 5 minutes. Mix the beans into the vegetables, a couple of spoonfuls at a time, mashing them roughly as you go. When all the beans have been added, season to taste and cook gently to heat through thoroughly.

RECIPE 2

In this recipe the fried beans are topped with tomatoes and cheese, grilled and served with poached or fried eggs to make a substantial meal.

8 oz (225 g) dried red kidney beans, soaked overnight in cold water

2 tablespoons (30 ml) olive oil

1 teaspoon cumin seeds

½ teaspoon ground cumin

1 teaspoon chilli powder

salt and black pepper to taste

2 large ripe tomatoes, thickly sliced

4 oz (100 g) Cheddar cheese, grated

4 eggs

Drain and rinse the beans under cold water. Put them into a saucepan and cover with 2 pints (1.2 litres) cold water. Bring to the boil, boil rapidly for 10 minutes, lower the heat and simmer gently, covered, for about 1 hour. The beans should be tender but not too soft and most of the liquid absorbed. Drain if necessary. Heat the oil in a saucepan. Add half of the beans, the cumin seeds and the ground cumin. Mash the rest of the beans roughly with a potato masher and add to the whole beans in the pan. Season with chilli powder, salt and pepper, stirring well. When heated through, put the beans on to a large heatproof dish. Smooth over and lay the sliced tomatoes on top. Now add the grated cheese and place the dish under a medium grill until the cheese melts and bubbles nicely. While this is going on, fry or poach the eggs and serve them on top.

Santa Clara Bean Loaf MEXICO

Serves 4

This is a very quick way to make a satisfying and filling meal.

1 × 14 oz (400 g) can of
  cooked red kidney beans
1 × 14 oz (400 g) can of
  cooked haricot beans
3 oz (75 g) fresh breadcrumbs
2 oz (50 g) sunflower seeds
2 oz (50 g) dry-roasted
  peanuts
1 small green bell pepper,
  seeded and cut into dice

1 medium onion, peeled and
  finely chopped
2 large tomatoes, skinned,
  seeded (see page 19) and
  roughly chopped
1 egg, beaten
salt and black pepper to taste
½ teaspoon prepared English
  mustard

Preheat the oven to 350°F (180°C, gas mark 4). Drain the beans, but reserve the liquid from the haricot beans only. Mash the beans together with a potato masher, add all the other ingredients and mix thoroughly. Pack into a 2 lb (900 g) greased loaf tin. Bake in the preheated oven for 45 minutes or until the loaf is firm to the touch. Cool in the tin for 10 minutes. Turn out and slice thickly. Serve with tomato ketchup or *pebre* sauce (see page 104) and a green salad.

Savoury Green Banana and MEXICO
Bean Layers (*Platano Verde con Capas de Judias*)

Serves 6

In this old colonial Spanish dish from Oaxaca in Mexico, the sweetness of the bananas marries well with the floury beans. This is good as a side dish or as a substitute for rice or potatoes.

8 oz (225 g) dried black beans,
　soaked overnight in cold
　water, drained, covered with
　fresh water and cooked until
　tender (see page 12)
1 tablespoon (15 ml) tomato
　purée, mixed with ¼ pint
　(150 ml) hot water
4 tablespoons (60 ml) olive oil
1 large onion, peeled and
　finely chopped
1 bay leaf
salt and ground black pepper
　to taste
6 green (unripe) bananas
4 oz (100 g) feta cheese,
　crumbled
3 oz (75 g) butter
2 eggs, beaten

Drain the beans and put in a blender or food processor with the tomato purée and hot water mixture. Blend to a purée. Heat the oil in a large saucepan and fry the onion in it until very soft. Add the bay leaf and the bean purée and cook, stirring, until it forms a soft but not too dry paste. Season to taste with salt and pepper and set aside.

Preheat the oven to 375°F (190°C, gas mark 5). Peel the bananas. Put them in a saucepan and cover with water. Bring to the boil, add some salt, reduce the heat and simmer, uncovered, for about 10–15 minutes or until they are tender. Drain and mash while they are still warm. Add the crumbled feta cheese and 2 oz (50 g) of the butter. Stir in the eggs and mix well. Butter an ovenproof dish and put in half the banana mixture. Cover with the bean paste and top with the remaining banana mix. Dot with the remaining butter and bake in the preheated oven for 30 minutes. Serve immediately.

RICE

Rice was taken to Spain and Portugal by the Moors and by the mid-fifteenth century it was cultivated all the way from Aragon to Naples. A century later, rice was one of the first crops to be introduced into South America by the conquistadores. Nowadays, it is one of the most important foods of Latin America. Both long and short grain varieties are grown.

Long grain rice, where the grain is about four to five times longer than it is wide, has a tendency to separate in cooking, resulting in a fluffy but still firm texture.

With medium and short grain rice, the grains are short, plump and rounded. When cooked they become moist and tend to stick together. Such varieties are best in moulded dishes and puddings.

In Peru, Colombia and Ecuador, rice is cooked drier than we are used to in Western Europe. It is called *arroz graneado*. In Mexico, rice cooked with tomatoes and garlic is served as a separate course, *sopa seca* or dry soup (see page 114), at the main meal of the day. In Brazil, dishes of baked moulded rice are served as accompaniments to a main course. Here we give two recipes for such dishes, one for rice baked with tomatoes and cheese and the other with eggs, cheese and olives (see page 112). Guatemalan rice is fried in oil with vegetables and then boiled (see page 114). Then there are rice croquettes from Brazil (see page 115), rice cooked in coconut milk from Colombia (see page 116), rice with sweetcorn (see page 117) and rice omelettes (see page 119). The variety is huge and as colourful as the people of Latin America.

In addition to the rice recipes, we have also included two using other grains, one based on quinoa (see pages 20 and 119) and the other for a noodle dish.

Brazilian Rice (*Arroz Brasilerio*)

Serves 4 as a side dish

This basic rice dish is an excellent accompaniment to a main dish. It is also the basis of the two baked rice recipes that follow.

8 oz (225 g) long grain white rice	2 tomatoes, skinned, seeded (see page 19) and chopped
3 tablespoons (45 ml) olive oil	½ pint (275 ml) boiling water
1 small onion, peeled and thinly sliced	salt

Wash and rinse the rice well. Drain. Heat the oil in a large saucepan and fry the onion and rice, stirring all the time, until the rice starts to make a swishing sound. This takes about 10 minutes over a low heat and is important in producing the dry final product. Add the tomatoes and the boiling water *carefully* (because the rice will spatter). Stir once and return to the heat. Bring to the boil. Turn down the heat and cover. Cook for 20–25 minutes, until all the water has evaporated and the rice is tender. Remove from the heat and uncover to let the steam escape. Season and serve.

Note: When properly cooked each grain of rice should be separate.

Baked Rice (*Arroz de Forno*)   BRAZIL

Serves 4 as a side dish

RECIPE 1
Here layers of cooked rice, egg, cheese and olives are arranged in an
ovenproof dish and baked in the oven.

1 recipe quantity of Brazilian
   Rice (see page 111)
4 hard-boiled eggs, shelled and
   sliced
8 oz (225 g) Edam cheese,
   sliced

2 oz (50 g) black olives, pitted
   and sliced
2 oz (50 g) Cheddar cheese,
   grated
freshly ground black pepper

Preheat the oven to 375°F (190°C, gas mark 5). Butter a gratin dish
and fill it with layers of cooked rice, hard-boiled egg, Edam cheese
and olives. Sprinkle grated cheese over the top and season with
black pepper. Bake in the preheated oven for 20 minutes or until
bubbling and hot.

RECIPE 2
This is a simpler, lighter version of the previous recipe.

1 quantity of Brazilian rice (see
   page 111)
1 × 14 oz (400 g) can of
   tomatoes

2 oz (50 g) fresh breadcrumbs
4 oz (100 g) Cheddar cheese,
   grated
freshly ground black pepper

Preheat the oven to 375°F (190°C, gas mark 5). Put the cooked rice
in a buttered gratin dish. Purée the tomatoes and mix with the
breadcrumbs and cheese. Season with black pepper. Spread this
mixture over the rice and bake in the preheated oven for about 25
minutes or until the top is browned.

Green Rice (*Arroz Verde*) MEXICO

Serves 4 as a side dish

Here onion, bell pepper, chilli pepper and garlic are grilled, combined with fresh herbs and lettuce and puréed. The resultant green and spicy sauce is then cooked with the rice.

8 oz (225 g) long grain white rice
1 onion, peeled and quartered
1 clove garlic, peeled and cut in half
1 green bell pepper, seeded and quartered
2 fresh green chilli peppers, seeded and halved
3 large cos lettuce leaves, chopped

1 oz (25 g) fresh parsley, chopped
1 oz (25 g) fresh coriander, chopped
½–¾ pint (275–450 ml) water
salt and ground black pepper to taste
3 tablespoons (45 ml) olive oil

Soak the rice in hot water for about 15 minutes. Meanwhile, place the onion, garlic, bell pepper and chilli peppers under a medium grill until blistered and soft. Remove the skin from the bell pepper (see page 13). Put the grilled vegetables in a blender or food processor with the lettuce, parsley, coriander and water. Season with salt and pepper and process to a thin purée. Heat the oil in a large saucepan, stir in the drained rice and fry until it is shiny and golden in colour. Tip the pan to one side, holding back the rice with a large spatula and drain off any excess oil. Add the puréed ingredients to the rice. Cover and cook over a moderate heat for 15–18 minutes, by which time holes will have appeared over the surface of the rice. Fork up, taste and adjust the seasoning. Replace the lid and leave to stand for about 20 minutes. It can be served as it is or it can be packed into a 2 pint (1.2 litre) ring mould, pressed down well with a wooden spoon and then turned out to serve. If you are not ready to serve immediately, it can be kept warm, covered in the ring mould, and turned out when you are.

Rice Guatemalan Style (*Arroz Guatemalteco*)

Serves 4 as a side dish

2 tablespoons (30 ml) olive oil
6 oz (175 g) long grain white
  rice
1 carrot, peeled and diced
1 stick celery, trimmed and cut
  into thin strips

1 small red bell pepper, seeded
  and cut into small dice
2 oz (50 g) fresh or frozen
  green peas
salt and black pepper to taste

Heat the oil in a large saucepan. Add the rice and stir constantly until the oil has been absorbed. Stir in all the prepared vegetables. Add ¾ pint (450 ml) of water and bring to the boil. Turn down the heat, cover and simmer for 15–20 minutes, or until the rice and vegetables are tender and all the liquid has been absorbed. Serve hot or cold.

Mexican Rice (*Arroz a la Mexicana*)

Serves 6–8

This rather elaborately garnished Mexican rice dish is served as a separate course called *sopa seca* (dry soup) before the main dish at the midday meal.

12 oz (350 g) long grain white
  rice
1 medium onion, peeled and
  chopped
1 clove garlic, peeled and
  crushed
1 lb (450 g) ripe tomatoes,
  skinned, seeded (see page
  19) and roughly chopped

3 tablespoons (45 ml) olive oil
1¼ pints (700 ml) vegetable
  stock
salt
4 oz (100 g) fresh or frozen
  green peas

GARNISH

3–4 red chilli peppers, sliced
  from tip to stem in 4–5
  sections to form 'flowers'

parsley sprigs
1 large avocado, stoned,
  peeled and sliced

Put the rice in a bowl. Cover it with hot water and leave to soak for 15 minutes. Drain it and rinse in cold water. Leave to dry off a little in the sieve. Put the onion, garlic and prepared tomatoes in a blender or food processor and process to a smooth purée. Leave to one side. Heat the olive oil in a large heavy saucepan. Put in the rice and stir-fry over a low heat until the oil is absorbed. Add the purée and the vegetable stock. Bring to the boil. Cover the pan and simmer over the lowest possible heat for 10–15 minutes or until the rice is tender. Add salt to taste and the peas. Cook for a further 5 minutes until the peas are cooked. Serve garnished with prepared chilli peppers, parsley sprigs and avocado slices.

Rice Croquettes (*Croquettes de Arroz*)   BRAZIL

Serves 4

Serve these croquettes on their own with a sauce (see pages 75–82) or as an accompaniment to another dish.

10 oz (275 g) rice, cooked and well drained

1 tablespoon (15 ml) tomato purée, diluted in 2 tablespoons (30 ml) hot water

3 eggs, separated

2 oz (50 g) Parmesan cheese

4 spring onions, trimmed and chopped

1 oz (25 g) butter, melted

1 tablespoon (15 ml) chopped fresh parsley

salt and black pepper to taste

corn oil or other vegetable oil for frying

Mix the rice, diluted tomato purée, egg yolks, Parmesan cheese, spring onions, butter and parsley together. Taste and season. Place the mixture in a pan and cook over a low heat until it is thick in texture. Cool completely. Beat the egg whites until frothy. Take small handfuls of the rice mixture and shape into croquettes. Roll in the beaten egg whites. Heat the oil in a frying pan and fry the croquettes until golden on all sides. Drain on absorbent kitchen paper and serve.

Moulded Rice (*Angu de Arroz*)   BRAZIL

Serves 6 as a side dish

Brazilians like to make these creamy moulded puddings from rice and coconut milk. They are served at room temperature as an accompaniment to the main dish.

12 oz (350 g) risotto rice,
   rinsed, drained and soaked
   overnight in cold water
¼ pint (450 ml) medium-thick
   coconut milk (see page 15 or
   use canned milk)

2 oz (50 g) butter
1 teaspoon salt

Put the rice and its soaking water in a saucepan, bring to the boil, cover, lower the heat and simmer for 20 minutes or until the liquid is absorbed and the rice is soft and swollen. Stir in the coconut milk and cook, mashing the rice with the back of a wooden spoon, for 2 minutes. Stir in the butter and season with a little salt. Turn into a buttered mould and allow to cool. Unmould by covering with a serving plate and turning quickly. Serve at room temperature.

Rice with Coconut and Raisins   COLOMBIA
(*Arroz con Coco y Pasas*)

Serves 6 as a side dish

This rice dish has the distinctive flavour of the Spanish Indian cuisine of Colombia, a style of cooking characterized by the use of coconut milk.

8 oz (225 g) raisins
1½ pints (900 ml) medium-
   thick coconut milk (see page
   15 or use canned milk)
1 oz (25 g) butter

1 small onion, peeled and
   grated
12 oz (350 g) long grain white
   rice
2 teaspoons sugar

Soak the raisins in the coconut milk for 30 minutes. Heat the butter in a saucepan and fry the onion until it is soft. Stir in the rice, making sure it absorbs the butter. Then add the raisins and coconut milk and the sugar. Bring to the boil, stir once, reduce the heat to the lowest possible simmer, cover and cook for 20–25 minutes until the rice is tender, fluffy and all the liquid has been taken up. Allow to stand for 10–15 minutes and mix through with a fork just before serving.

Rice with Sweetcorn
(*Arroz Blanco con Elote*)

MEXICO

Serves 4 as a side dish

This dish may be prepared and served immediately or prepared ahead of time, then pressed into a 2 pint (1.2 litre) ring mould or ovenproof serving dish and covered with foil, ready to bake in a pre-heated oven at 350°F (180°C, gas mark 4) for 25–30 minutes just before serving.

8 oz (225 g) long grain white rice
1 small onion, peeled and quartered
1 clove garlic, peeled
¾ pint (450 ml) vegetable stock or water

salt and black pepper to taste
4 tablespoons (60 ml) olive oil
5 oz (150 g) fresh or frozen sweetcorn

Pour boiling water over the rice and leave to soak for about 15 minutes. Drain and rinse well in cold water. Shake dry. In a blender or food processor, blend the onion, garlic and stock or water. Season with salt and pepper. In a large saucepan, heat the oil until very hot and put in the drained rice. Take care because the rice will splatter. Fry, stirring from time to time, for about 10 minutes until the rice is shiny and golden coloured. Tip the rice to one side and drain off any excess oil. Now pour on the onion, garlic and stock mixture, cover and cook gently for 15 minutes. Small holes will have appeared on the surface of the rice. Add the sweetcorn and cook, covered, for a further 5 minutes until the corn and rice are tender. Leave to rest covered for 20 minutes before serving.

Rice with Greens (*Arroz con Col*)

BRAZIL

Serves 4

In Brazil this dish would normally be made with turnip tops. However, since they are not that common here, we have suggested using spring greens or Savoy cabbage instead.

6 tablespoons (90 ml) olive oil
1 medium onion, peeled and
  sliced
1 medium carrot, peeled and
  grated
8 oz (225 g) risotto rice,
  washed and drained

1 pint (550 ml) vegetable stock
  or water
salt and black pepper to taste
4 oz (100 g) spring greens or
  Savoy cabbage, cut into
  narrow strips

Heat 3 tablespoons (45 ml) of the oil in a saucepan, add the onion
and carrot and cook until the onion is softened. Add the rice and
cook gently for 5 minutes, turning until all the grains are coated with
oil. Add the vegetable stock or water, cover and cook over a gentle
heat for about 20–25 minutes until the rice is tender and all the liquid has been absorbed. Season to taste. Heat the remaining 3 tablespoons (45 ml) of oil in a frying pan, add the strips of spring greens
or Savoy cabbage and fry for 5 minutes. Strain off any oil and add
the greens to the rice mixture. Mix well and serve.

Rice and Pea Pudding   BRAZIL
(*Arroz e Ervilhas em Pudim*)

Serves 4

4 oz (100 g) butter
8 oz (225 g) risotto rice,
  washed and drained
1 pint (550 ml) vegetable stock
  or water
2 medium onions, peeled and
  sliced

4 oz (100 g) feta cheese, in
  small chunks
8 oz (225 g) fresh or frozen
  green peas
4 eggs, beaten
salt and black pepper to taste

In a saucepan, melt 2 oz (50 g) of the butter, add the rice and cook
gently, turning frequently, for about 5 minutes. Add the stock, cover
and cook gently for about 25–30 minutes until the rice is tender and
all the liquid has been absorbed. While the rice is cooking, heat the
remaining butter in a frying pan and fry the onions in it until soft.
Then, 10 minutes before the rice has finished cooking, add the
onions and feta cheese to the rice. Cook the peas in boiling water
until tender and drain. Preheat the oven to 440°F (230°C, gas mark
8). When the rice, onion and cheese mixture has finally cooked, add
the peas and eggs. Mix well and season to taste. Pour the mixture
into a greased ovenproof dish and bake in the preheated oven for
about 10–15 minutes, until the eggs have just set.

Rice and Tomato Omelettes BRAZIL
(*Omelettes com Tomate e Arroz*)

Serves 4

In Brazil, an omelette is generally not filled, but served with the filling placed around it.

4 oz (100 g) butter	3 tablespoons (45 ml) olive oil
2 medium onions, peeled and finely chopped	1 clove garlic, peeled and crushed
6 oz (175 g) long grain white rice	8 oz (225 g) tomatoes, skinned (see page 19) and chopped
¼ pint (450 ml) vegetable stock or water	4 parsley sprigs, chopped
salt and black pepper to taste	8 eggs

Melt 1 oz (25 g) of the butter in a saucepan, add half of the chopped onion and cook gently until soft and golden. Add the rice, stirring well until all the grains are covered by the butter. Pour in the stock or water and add 2 oz (50 g) butter. Cover and cook over a very gentle heat for about 25–30 minutes until the rice is tender and all the liquid has been absorbed. Season to taste.

While the rice is cooking, prepare the tomato mixture and the omelettes. Heat the olive oil in a saucepan, add the remaining chopped onion and the crushed clove of garlic and cook over a gentle heat until soft and golden. Add the tomatoes and simmer, uncovered, for about 20–25 minutes until the liquid has almost evaporated. Stir in the parsley and season to taste. Keep warm.

Beat the eggs together in a large bowl and season lightly. Heat the remaining butter in a large frying pan and pour in a quarter of the egg mixture. Cook over a low heat until firm. Fold the omelette in half in the pan, cook a little longer, then set aside and keep warm. Use the remaining egg mixture to make three more omelettes in the same way. Serve the omelettes with the warm rice mixture on one side and the warm tomato mixture on the other.

Quinoa Chowder (*Chupe de Quinoa*) PERU

Serves 4

Quinoa is a tiny golden-coloured grain with a delicate flavour. It is easy to digest and has a high nutritional value. The Incas called it the 'mother grain' and thought very highly of it. Quinoa has a bitter tasting coating and should always be thoroughly rinsed in cold water before cooking.

5 oz (150 g) quinoa
2 tablespoons (30 ml) olive oil
2 cloves garlic, peeled and
    crushed
1 green chilli pepper, seeded
    and finely chopped
pinch of ground cumin
salt and black pepper to taste
1½ pints (900 ml) water

8 oz (225 g) potatoes, peeled
    and roughly chopped
4 oz (100 g) feta cheese, cut
    into small cubes
8 oz (225 g) fresh spinach,
    washed and cut into shreds
1 hard-boiled egg, shelled and
    sliced

Rinse the quinoa thoroughly in cold running water. Put into a saucepan with plenty of cold water. Bring to the boil, stirring now and then, lower the heat and simmer for 10 minutes or until the quinoa is tender. Drain and rinse once more. Set aside. In a saucepan, heat the olive oil, add the garlic and chilli pepper and fry for 1–2 minutes. Add the cumin, salt and pepper to taste and the water. Bring to the boil and add the chopped potatoes and the cooked quinoa. Cook on a medium heat for about 10–15 minutes until the potatoes are tender. Stir in the feta cheese and the shredded spinach. Correct the seasoning and cook for a further 2 minutes. Serve hot, garnished with the slices of hard-boiled egg.

Variation Omit the potatoes and add 1 lb (450 g) of shelled broad beans.

# Sesame Noodles (*Fideos con Ajonjolí*)					PERU

Serves 4

The Chinese came to Peru in the mid-nineteenth century and Lima now has one of the world's largest Chinatowns. This recipe demonstrates the Chinese influence on Peruvian cooking and vice versa.

1 lb (450 g) dried fettucine
    noodles
4 oz (100 g) butter
1 tablespoon (15 ml) olive oil
2 cloves garlic, peeled and
    crushed

1 red chilli pepper, seeded and
    chopped
2 oz (50 g) sesame seeds

Bring 2½ pints (1.5 litres) water to the boil in a large saucepan. Add the fettucine and cook for 8–10 minutes until tender (*al dente*).

Remove from the heat, drain and add 1 oz (25 g) of the butter and the olive oil. Toss well and set aside in a warm place. Heat the remaining 3 oz (75 g) of butter in a saucepan. Add the crushed garlic and the red chilli pepper and cook gently until the garlic is soft and golden. Remove from the heat and cool a little. Pour the flavoured butter through a fine sieve over the noodles, pressing out the flavour from the garlic and pepper. Mix gently, cover and set aside in a warm place. In a dry frying pan, roast the sesame seeds over a fairly high heat for a few minutes. They will turn golden and start to jump. Mix half the seeds into the noodles and sprinkle the remainder on top to serve.

Puddings and Sweets

A bowl laden with fruit is the customary dessert in Latin America. This does not mean, however, that South Americans do not have a sweet tooth. Puddings, pastries, pastelitos and poached fruits do play a role, but not normally as part of a meal. They are eaten mid-morning with coffee, at four o'clock in the afternoon with tea (*onces*) or as a snack before bedtime. There is very little native tra-dition of sweet-making and most of the now-popular sweet dishes were introduced or created in the colonial period by the Spanish in Peru and Mexico and by the Portuguese in Brazil, where the lavish use of egg yolks, almonds and sugar in desserts is very much the result of Portuguese influence. Even today the Spanish and Por-tuguese Catholic convents of Latin America make the very best sweets for sale. They compete furiously with one another to main-tain their culinary reputations (and income!).

Chilled Bread Pudding (*Charcada*)

Serves 4

1 thick slice of soft white bread, crust removed	8 oz (225 g) caster sugar
2 tablespoons (30 ml) milk	4 fl oz (100 ml) water
2 oz (50 g) raisins	3 egg yolks
juice of ½ large orange	2 oz (50 g) ground almonds

Break up the bread into very small pieces and soak in the milk for 15 minutes. Drain and squeeze gently. Soak the raisins in the orange juice until plumped up. Drain but reserve the orange juice. Put the sugar and water into a saucepan. Bring to the boil over a moderate heat and boil gently until the sugar has dissolved. Remove from the heat and cool. Beat the egg yolks and add them to the cooled sugar solution together with the ground almonds, bread and raisins. Reheat the mixture and cook gently until it thickens, about 10 minutes. Remove from the heat and stir in the reserved orange juice. Pour into individual serving bowls and chill prior to serving.

Papaya with Blackcurrant Sauce (*Papaya con Salsa de Casis*)

Serves 4

Ripe papayas have a smooth green to yellow skin with pink luscious flesh. In this recipe the sharpness of the blackcurrants combines very well with the flesh of this sweet Latin American fruit.

8 oz (225 g) blackcurrants	GARNISH
4 tablespoons (60 ml) icing sugar	4 small bunches of blackcurrants
4 fl oz (100 ml) double cream, whipped	fresh mint leaves
4 ripe papayas, peeled, halved and seeded	

Purée the blackcurrants in a blender or food processor with the icing sugar. Strain on to the whipped cream and fold in. Put in the refrigerator. Slice the papaya halves lengthways. Arrange the slices on 4 small serving plates and chill until needed. Just prior to serving, spoon the fruit cream over the papaya slices. Garnish with the bunches of blackcurrants and mint leaves.

Grilled Pineapple in Rum Sauce
(*Piña a la Parrilla en Salsa de Ron*)

Serves 4

This is a very good way to serve a pineapple that may be less than perfectly ripe and fragrant.

1 medium pineapple, about
    3 lb (1.4 kg)
4 oz (100 g) soft brown sugar
½ teaspoon ground cinnamon

¼ teaspoon ground cloves
4 tablespoons (60 ml) dark
    rum

Preheat the grill to high. Cut off 1 in (2.5 cm) from the base and top of the pineapple. Keep the top. Cut off the skin evenly and remove any 'eyes'. Slice the pineapple across into four even slices. Remove the hard central core with an apple corer. Put the pineapple slices in a shallow flameproof dish in one layer. Combine the sugar, cinnamon and cloves in a bowl. Sprinkle half this mixture evenly over the pineapple slices. Put them under the grill, as near to the heat as possible. Grill them quickly until they are lightly golden, about 6–8 minutes. Remove from under the grill and turn the slices over. Sprinkle with the remaining sugar and spice mixture and place under the grill for a further 5 minutes. Arrange the grilled fruit slices on a serving dish. Add the rum and 1 tablespoon (15 ml) water to the dish in which the pineapple was grilled. Place over a low heat and stir until bubbling, scraping up all the caramelized sugar from the dish. Pour through a sieve over the sliced pineapple. Garnish with the reserved pineapple top and serve.

Almond Caramel Custard   MEXICO
(*Flan de Almendra*)

Serves 4

This was originally Spanish, but is now Mexico's favourite pudding.

5 oz (125 g) caster sugar
¾ pint (450 ml) milk
4 egg yolks

½ teaspoon vanilla essence
pinch of salt
1½ oz (40 g) ground almonds

Preheat the oven to 350°F (180°C, gas mark 4). In a small heavy saucepan, gently heat 2 oz (50 g) of the sugar, swirling constantly, until it melts and turns a rich golden brown. Have ready a 1 pint (550 ml) mould, warmed by standing in hot water. Pour the caramelized sugar into the mould, turning it in all directions so that it coats the bottom and part of the sides. Set aside. Bring the milk to the boil. Remove from the heat and cool. Beat the remaining sugar with the egg yolks until thick and creamy. Gradually add the milk, vanilla essence, salt and almonds. Mix well. Pour this mixture into the prepared mould. Place the mould in a tin or ovenproof dish filled with hot water to reach half-way up the sides of the mould and bake for 1 hour in the preheated oven, or until a knife inserted into the custard comes out clean. Cool, then chill in the refrigerator. To unmould, run a knife around the custard and turn out, upside down, on to a serving dish. Serve. The caramel will have by now become a wickedly sweet sauce!

Sweet Stuffed Chayotes (*Chayotes Rellenos*)   MEXICO

Serves 4

The chayote is a pear-shaped member of the squash family (see page 54). In this traditional Mexican dish it is stuffed with a sort of fruit cake mix.

2 chayotes	3 oz (75 g) raisins
2 eggs	6 tablespoons (90 ml) sherry
3 oz (75 g) sugar	2 oz (50 g) ground almonds
½ teaspoon ground nutmeg	2 oz (50 g) flaked almonds
4 oz (100 g) sponge cake crumbs	

Boil the chayotes in their skins for about 30 minutes. Halve and carefully scoop the flesh and seeds out, leaving a ½ in (1.2 cm) shell. Mash the flesh with the seeds and leave to cool. Reserve the shells. Preheat the oven to 350°F (180°C, gas mark 4). Blend the eggs, sugar, nutmeg and chayote pulp together. Mix this purée with the cake crumbs, then stir in the raisins and sherry. Add the ground almonds, then spoon this mixture into the reserved chayote shells. Sprinkle with the flaked almonds and bake in the preheated oven for 30 minutes. Serve warm or cold with some whipped cream.

Chilled Peaches in Hot Syrup
(*Melocotones en Salsa Picante*)

Serves 4

Even sweet dishes do not escape the fire of chilli pepper in Latin America. In this dish, peaches are poached, chilled and served in a cold syrup spiced with chilli.

8 small (or 4 large) unripe peaches	8 allspice berries
	1 bay leaf
4 oz (100 g) caster sugar	1 in (2.5 cm) piece of root
1 pinch saffron threads (optional)	ginger, peeled and cut into 3 slices
1 dried red chilli pepper	1 pint (550 ml) cold water

Carefully peel all the peaches and set them aside. In a saucepan, combine the sugar, saffron if using, chilli pepper, allspice, bay leaf, ginger and water. Bring to the boil, lower the heat and simmer for 10 minutes. Add the peaches and poach them gently for about 20–30 minutes, depending on their size, or until tender when pierced with a skewer. Remove gently to a serving dish and set aside. Continue to simmer the syrup over a medium heat until it has reduced to about ½ pint (275 ml). With a slotted spoon, remove and discard the bay leaf, ginger and most of the allspice berries. Pour the hot syrup over the peaches, along with the chilli pepper, saffron threads and a few allspice berries. Chill thoroughly and serve.

Orange Pudding (*Pudim de Laranja*) BRAZIL

Serves 4

3 eggs	12 oz (350 g) caster sugar
7 egg yolks	juice of 3 large oranges

Preheat the oven to 325°F (170°C, gas mark 3). In a large bowl, beat all the ingredients together with a balloon whisk or an electric whisk until light and well increased in volume, about 10 minutes. Leave to rest for 30 minutes to allow the bubbles to subside. Grease a large soufflé dish and pour in the mixture. Place the dish in a tin or ovenproof dish of hot water, so that the water comes half-way up the sides of the soufflé dish. Cook in the preheated oven for about 1 hour, until the pudding is just firm throughout. Cool before serving.

Pears in Sparkling Wine
(*Peritas en Champaña*)

Serves 4

The final result of this pudding depends on the quality of the wine.
It need not be champagne but should be of decent quality.

4 large unripe pears, such as Williams or Doyenne du Comice	4 oz (100 g) caster sugar
	1 cinnamon stick, about 2 in (5 cm) long
1 pint (550 ml) dry sparkling wine	6 juniper berries
	1 dried red chilli pepper

With a vegetable peeler, carefully peel each pear, leaving the stalk
attached. Put the pears in a saucepan, with the wine, sugar, cinnamon stick, juniper berries and chilli pepper. Bring to the boil, then
lower the heat and gently simmer the pears for about 25–30 minutes
or until the pears are tender. Transfer the pears, carefully, to a serving bowl. Continue to cook the syrup until reduced to about ½ pint
(275 ml). Pour the hot syrup over the pears, along with the cinnamon stick, chilli pepper and a few juniper berries (discard the rest).
Serve chilled.

Variation Omit the juniper berries and poach the pears in ½ pint
(275 ml) red wine and ¼ pint (150 ml) port.

Poached Figs (*Higos en Almíbar*)

Serves 4

The leaves of figs are very fragrant and if you can get them, add
them to the poaching liquid and omit the spices. Once the syrup
has reduced, discard the leaves.

8 fresh firm figs	1 piece of cinnamon stick, about 2 in (5 cm)
8 oz (225 g) caster sugar	
8 juniper berries	1½ pints (900 ml) water
8 allspice berries	

Wipe the figs gently with a soft dry cloth and set aside. In a
saucepan, combine the sugar, juniper and allspice berries and cinnamon stick with the water. Bring to the boil, lower the heat and simmer for 20 minutes. Add the figs gently and poach for another 20
minutes. Transfer the figs to a serving dish and set aside. Continue

to simmer the poaching syrup until reduced to about ½ pint (275 ml). Pour over the figs, along with the cinnamon stick and a few of the juniper and allspice berries (discard the rest). Serve chilled.

Pumpkin Pudding (*Dolce de Abobora*)

Serves 4

3 eggs
pinch of salt
4 oz (100 g) soft brown sugar
½ teaspoon ground cinnamon

¼ teaspoon ground cloves
1 lb (450 g) cooked mashed
   pumpkin, canned or fresh
¼ pint (150 ml) single cream

Preheat the oven to 350°F (180°C, gas mark 4). Break the eggs into a bowl and beat them lightly. Add the salt, sugar and spices. Whisk again. Stir in the pumpkin and cream. Pour the mixture into a greased 1 pint (550 ml) ovenproof dish. Place in a pan of hot water so that the water comes half-way up the sides of the dish. Bake in the preheated oven for about 1 hour or until a knife inserted into the pudding comes out clean. Serve warm.

Rice Pudding (*Arroz Dulce*)

Serves 4

This is a very popular Latin American pudding.

4 oz (100 g) pudding (round-
   grained) rice
pinch of salt
1 pint (550 ml) milk
several parings of lemon rind
1 cinnamon stick, about 2 in
   (5 cm) long

4 oz (100 g) caster sugar
3 egg yolks
1 oz (25 g) butter
powdered cinnamon, to
   decorate

Add the rice to some boiling salted water. Boil hard for 10 minutes. In another saucepan, bring the milk to the boil with the lemon rind and cinnamon stick. Drain the rice and add it to the milk. Allow to cook gently for 5 minutes, then remove from the heat and take out the lemon rind and cinnamon stick. Stir in the sugar. Beat the egg yolks and add them with the butter. Put back on to a gentle heat and cook, stirring continuously, until the mixture thickens slightly. Do not let it boil. Pour into individual serving bowls and sprinkle with powdered cinnamon. Serve cold.

Jicama Sweetmeats (*Golosinas de Jicama*)

Makes about 20

Jicamas are popular throughout South America but especially in Mexico. They are highly adaptable fruits, with a crisp juicy texture and a slight pear-like flavour. They can usually be found in Chinese food shops.

4 oz (100 g) jicama, grated	2 fl oz (50 ml) orange juice
1 oz (25 g) desiccated coconut	4 oz (100 g) caster sugar

Put all the ingredients in a saucepan and stir continuously over a low heat until the sugar is dissolved and the mixture quite liquid. Increase the heat and, still stirring, cook until the liquid is reduced and the mixture becomes sticky. Take heaped teaspoonfuls of the mixture and make little mounds on a sheet of foil that has been lightly brushed with corn or vegetable oil. Allow to cool. Store in an airtight container.

Quince Sweetmeats (*Membrillo*)   VENEZUELA

Makes about 50 pieces

2 lb (900 g) quinces, washed, peeled, cored and sliced	juice of 1 lemon
	granulated sugar

Put the quinces and lemon juice in a saucepan. Just cover with water. Bring to the boil and simmer until the fruit is soft. Strain and purée in a blender or food processor. To each 5 oz (150 g) of purée add an equal quantity of sugar. Return to a saucepan and stir over a low heat until the sugar is dissolved. Bring to a simmer and cook for 30–40 minutes, stirring from time to time. When the purée leaves the sides of the pan and is darker in colour, beat well and pour into a shallow baking tray. Leave to dry for about 3 days at room temperature. Slice into diamond shapes, dip in sugar, and wrap in waxed paper. Store in an airtight container.

Yautia Fritters

Serves 4

This sweet South American snack can also be served as a side dish to a savoury main course. We know yautia in Britain as eddoe or dasheen and it can be bought in West Indian food shops.

1 lb (450 g) raw yautia (eddoe or dasheen), grated
1 egg
½ teaspoon salt
grated peel of 1 lime
2 oz (50 g) cream cheese
1 tablespoon (15 ml) sugar
vegetable oil for deep-frying

Combine all the ingredients except the vegetable oil and mix well together. Heat the oil and deep-fry tablespoonfuls of the mixture, three or four at a time, until golden brown. Drain on absorbent kitchen paper and keep warm. Serve as soon as all the fritters are cooked.

Drinks

Latin America has a wide variety of drinks. Many are native to the area, such as drinking chocolate, tequila (a kind of cactus whisky, distilled from the agave family of succulents), *pisco* (a brandy from Peru), *pulque*, *chicha* and *tepache* (all fermented beer-like drinks) and *mate*, the most famous non-alcoholic drink of South America.

Mate is prepared in the same way as tea or herbal infusions. It is derived from the South American evergreen *Ilex paraguayensis*, a type of holly. It is drunk either hot or cold. Served cold, it is made double strength and served over ice, without milk but with sugar or lemon. *Mate* is readily available in the UK from healthfood shops. Tea itself is not so popular in Latin America, but it is drunk in Chile, usually with little sweet cakes.

German settlers introduced beer-making skills to Latin America and there are many very good beers. Winemaking was introduced by a variety of settlers including the Portuguese, Spanish, French and Italians. One bottle in every ten of the world's wine is produced in South America. Chile and Argentina produce the best and per-haps most well-known wines.

Brazil's coffee is considered to be the finest in the world, while very high quality coffees come from Colombia, Costa Rica and Mexico. Breakfast coffee is drunk with milk, but during the rest of the day it is taken black, strong and very sweet, served in little cups. Drinking chocolate is also popular, especially in Mexico, where it is drunk sweet with added spices such as cinnamon and cloves.

Breakfast Coffee (*Café de Desayuno*)

In Latin America coffee with milk (*cafe con leche* or *cafe com leite* in Brazil) is the standard way to serve coffee at breakfast. To prepare, make a pint of coffee *quadruple* strength and heat milk separately, almost to boiling point. Fill cups one-third full with coffee, then top up with the hot milk and serve.

After-Dinner Coffee (*Café de Olla*)

Serves 4–6

1¼ pints (700 ml) water
3 oz (75 g) dark brown sugar
2 in (5 cm) piece of cinnamon
  stick

4 cloves
2 oz (50 g) fresh coffee, finely
  ground

Put the water, sugar and spices in a pan and bring to the boil. Add the coffee, bring back to the boil, lower the heat and simmer for 2 minutes. Stir, cover and leave at the side of the stove for a few minutes so that the coffee grounds settle. Pour through a strainer into little coffee cups and serve.

Mexican Hot Chocolate (*Chocolate Mexicano*)

In Mexico hot chocolate is served spiced. Make hot drinking chocolate in the usual way using milk. Then to every 1 pint (550 ml), stir in ¼ teaspoon each of ground cinnamon and ground cloves. Whip until frothy and serve.

Champurrado

Serves 4

Champurrado is a gruel-like chocolate drink made with milk and raw *masa* (tortilla dough). A simple but almost as delicious Europeanized version can be made using cocoa powder and cornmeal. Champurrado is traditionally served during fiesta times, accompanied by tamales (see page 93).

1 pint (550 ml) milk or ½ pint (275 ml) milk and ½ pint (275 ml) water

2 tablespoons (30 ml) cocoa powder

2 tablespoons (30 ml) cornmeal

4 teaspoons sugar

1 teaspoon ground cinnamon

Whisk everything together and cook over a low heat in a double boiler or in a heatproof basin over a pan of simmering water for 30 minutes. Pour into cups and serve.

Chicha

Serves 8–10

Chicha is a native alcoholic drink which has been made in the same way for many hundreds of years. It is popular from Mexico to Paraguay. Today in Panama the word *chicha* in fact describes any drink; orange juice for instance is *chicha de naranja*. The women of an Indian tribe would traditionally be in charge of the chicha preparation. An *olla* or pot would be filled with masticated corn kernels or *masa* (corn mush). This would be allowed to ferment for 3 days before filtering and pressing. The following recipe makes a more (to Western taste anyway) appealing and palatable pineapple-based chicha.

1 large pineapple
2 lb (900 g) sugar
6 pints (3.3 litres) water
6 limes, thinly sliced

¼ teaspoon each ground cinnamon, cloves and nutmeg

Peel the pineapple and cut the peel into small sections. Roughly chop then mash the pulp. Dissolve the sugar in the water, then add all the other ingredients including the pineapple peel and pulp. Allow the mixture to stand, covered, for 1–2 days in a clay bowl or other vessel until it takes on a sharp cider-like taste. Strain and keep in the refrigerator until needed. Serve chilled. The alcoholic content is variable, so, at least initially, drink in moderation.

Hot Toasted Corn Drink Mix (*Pinole*)

This is a Peublo Indian recipe from New Mexico. It makes a good cocoa powder substitute.

1 lb (450 g) cornmeal
8 oz (225 g) sugar

1 teaspoon cinnamon powder

Spread the cornmeal in a thin layer over a baking sheet. Brown in a hot oven at 425°F (220°C, gas mark 7) for 8–10 minutes, stirring around from time to time to prevent scorching. Cool, put in a bowl and add the sugar and cinnamon. Store in an airtight tin. Stir into hot milk in the same proportions as cocoa, according to taste, and simmer for about 15 minutes before consumption.

Margarita

Serves 2

The classic way to drink tequila is to sprinkle salt on the wrist, toss it down, take a swallow of tequila and chase it with a bite of lime or lemon. Margarita is a drink which was designed to simulate the tequila taste without the ritual. It has now become a classic in its own right.

juice of 1 lime and the lime
 skins
salt in a saucer

2 fl oz (50 ml) tequila
1 fl oz (25 ml) triple sec
cracked ice

Moisten the rims of two glasses with the lime skins. Then dip the rims into the saucer of salt until lightly frosted. Shake the tequila, triple sec and lime juice together with the cracked ice. Pour into the glasses and drink.

Rompope   MEXICO

Serves 4

This is a sort of egg nog produced in Tenancingo. It is eaten like ice-cream by children and women. The men mix it, as here, with rum or brandy.

1 pint (550 ml) milk	6 measures of rum
4 oz (100 g) sugar	3 egg yolks
pinch each of ground cinnamon, nutmeg and cloves	dash of vanilla essence

Boil the milk, sugar and spices together until thick. Remove from the heat and cool. When cool, stir in the rum slowly. Beat the egg yolks with the vanilla essence until thick and creamy. Pour the milk and rum mixture on to the egg yolks, slowly whisking constantly with a balloon whisk. Serve.

Sangría

Serves 2–4

juice of 2 limes	ice cubes
2 pints (1.2 litres) orange juice	fresh mint sprigs
1 pint (550 ml) dry red wine	

Put all the ingredients, except for the ice cubes and mint sprigs, into a large glass jug. Mix well with a long spoon. Put in plenty of ice cubes and garnish with the mint. Serve.

Sangrita de Chapala

Serves 1–2

Sangrita is usually served cold as an aperitif, but it also has an affinity with tequila. Some sip it after each swallow of tequila, while others mix 1 part tequila to 4 parts sangrita to make a cocktail.

½ pint (275 ml) orange juice	½ teaspoon tabasco sauce
3 tablespoons (45 ml) grenadine syrup	pinch of salt

Shake everything together well. Chill and serve.

Tepache

Makes 1¼ pints (750 ml)

This tangy and refreshing pineapple and barley drink is not unlike our own lemon-barley water.

1 large pineapple	8 whole cloves
cold water	1 lb (450 g) pot barley
1 large piece of cinnamon bark	3 lb (1.4 kg) brown sugar

Crush the pineapple, skin and all, and cover with 5 pints (2.75 litres) cold water. Put in a large clay crock or glass bowl. Add the spices, cover, and allow to stand for 2 days. On the second day, boil the barley and sugar in 1½ pints (900 ml) water until the cereal swells and cracks. Drain and add the barley water to the pineapple mash. Leave to stand for another 2 days. Finally, strain well through a muslin-lined sieve over plenty of ice in a punch bowl and serve.

Suppliers

Most of the ingredients mentioned in this book are widely available in food stores and supermarkets. However, for more unusual goods the following addresses may be useful:

La Mexicana
17 Faraday Road
Rabans Lane
Aylesbury
Buckinghamshire
HP19 3RY
Tel: 0296 84243

Mexicolore
28 Warriner Gardens
London SW11 4EB
Tel: 071 622 9577

Garcia and Sons
248 Portobello Road
London W11 1LL
Tel: 071 221 6119

Lourdes Nichols
Chimalistac
Upper Hollis
Great Missenden
Buckinghamshire
Tel: 02406 4348

Panzers Delicatessen
13-19 Circus Road
St Johns Wood
London NW8 9TS
Tel: 071 722 8596

The Cool Chile Company
Unit 7
34 Bassett Road
London W10 6JL
Tel: 081 968 8898
(Imports fresh and dried chillies from California and Mexico, and delivers by post)

Notes for American Cooks

ENGLISH-AMERICAN FOOD AND COOKING TERMS

Some of the main food and cooking terms used in the text are given below with their American equivalent:

ENGLISH	AMERICAN
aubergine	eggplant
baking sheet	cookie sheet
baking tin	cake pan
castor sugar	granulated white sugar
chilli powder	chilli seasoning
cooking fat	shortening
courgette	zucchini
currant	raisin
demerara sugar	dark brown sugar
desiccated coconut	shredded coconut
French bean	snap or string bean
frying pan	skillet
to grill	to broil
hard-boiled egg	hard-cooked egg
icing sugar	confectioner's sugar
marrow	squash
to mince	to grind
pinch of	dash of
plain flour	white flour
prawn	shrimp
to shell	to hull
to sieve	to strain
spring onion	scallion
to stone or seed	to pit
swede	rutabaga
tin	can
treacle	molasses

ENGLISH-AMERICAN MEASUREMENTS

ENGLISH	AMERICAN
Liquid	
1 fl oz	1½ tablespoons (⅛ cup)
4 fl oz	¼ pint (½ cup)
8 fl oz	½ pint (1 cup)
16 fl oz	1 pint (2 cups)
20 fl oz (1 pint)	1¼ pints (2½ cups)

Dry Measurements

FLOUR

1 oz	4 tablespoons (¼ cup)
2 oz	8 tablespoons (½ cup)
4 oz	1 cup

BUTTER, SUGAR

1 oz	2 tablespoons (⅛ cup)
2 oz	4 tablespoons (¼ cup)
8 oz	1 cup

You will also find the following cup conversion list of specific foods useful:

1 cup measure contains the following:

6 oz	apple, chopped	2½ oz	cabbage, shredded
5 oz	artichoke (sunchoke), grated	4 oz	carrot, grated
		7 oz	cauliflower, chopped
5¼ oz	asparagus tips	4 oz	celery, chopped
		8 oz	cheese, cottage
6 oz	barley, cooked	4 oz	cheese, grated
7 oz	beans, dried	7 oz	chickpeas (garbanzos)
4½ oz	beans, green	2¼ oz	coconut, dried
6 oz	black-eyed peas	2 oz	coriander leaves, chopped
4 oz	breadcrumbs		
7 oz	broccoli, chopped	6 oz	sweetcorn, fresh
3½ oz	buckwheat flour	4 oz	cornmeal
5½ oz	bulgar wheat	5½ oz	cracked wheat
8 oz	butter	4 oz	croûtons
		6 oz	cucumber, sliced

6 oz	dates, chopped	5 oz	potatoes, cooked, diced
8 fl oz	dressings, salad		
		7½ oz	potatoes, mashed
5 oz	gluten flour	3½ oz	prunes, stewed
7 oz	haricot (navy) beans	5 oz	raisins
2 oz	herbs, chopped	6½ oz	rice, brown
12 oz	honey	5¾ oz	rice, wild
		4 oz	rice flour, brown
8 oz	lentils, dried	4½ oz	rye flour
7¼ oz	lentils, sprouted		
6½ oz	Lima beans	8 fl oz	sauces
8 fl oz	liquids	3½ oz	sesame seeds
		6½ oz	soybeans, cooked
8 oz	margarine	7½ oz	soybeans, dried
4 oz	milk, dried	3 oz	soy flour
8 fl oz	milk, liquid	7 oz	soy grits, cooked
5 oz	mixed vegetables	5 oz	soy grits, dried
12 oz	molasses	4½ oz	squash, chopped
2½ oz	mushrooms, chopped	5¼ oz	strawberries
		5 oz	sunflower seeds
5 oz	nuts, chopped		
		7 oz	tomatoes, chopped or canned
4 oz	oatmeal, cooked		
2¾ oz	oats, rolled	8 oz	tomato purée
8 fl oz	oil		
4 oz	okra, sliced	5 oz	vegetables, chopped
4 oz	olives, sliced		
6 oz	onion, sliced	8 fl oz	water
6 oz	oranges, diced	1¾ oz	wheat bran
		5½ oz	wheat, cracked
2 oz	parsley, chopped	2½ oz	wheat germ
6 oz	pasta, cooked	6 oz	wheat grains, sprouted or cooked
5¼ oz	pastry flour		
9¼ oz	peanut butter	4¼ oz	wholewheat flour
7 oz	peas, dried, whole or split	6 oz	wholewheat pasta
		5¼ oz	wholewheat pastry flour
5 oz	peas, green		
4 oz	pepper, green, diced		
7 oz	pinto beans	8 fl oz	yoghurt

Bibliography

Booth, George C., *The Food and Drink of Mexico*, Dover, 1964

Brown, Cora, *South American Cookbook*, Dover, 1972

Grace, Vilma J., *Latin American and Cholesterol Conscious Cooking*, Acropolis, 1979

Harris, Jessica B., *Tasting Brazil*, Macmillan, 1992

Hughes, Phyllis, *Pueblo Indian Cookbook*, Museum of New Mexico Press, 1977

Karoff, Barbara, *South American Cooking: Food and Feasts from the New World*, Addison Wesley, 1990

Kennedy, Diane, *The Tortilla Book*, Harper and Row, 1975

Latin American Cooking, Time Life, 1970

Ortiz, Elizabeth L., *Book of Latin American Cooking*, Penguin, 1991

Ortiz, Elizabeth L., *Little Brazilian Cookbook*, Appletree, 1992

Rosas-Lombardi, Felipe, *The Art of Latin American Cooking*, Harper Collins, 1991

Spieler, Marlena, *Flavours of Mexico*, Grafton Books, 1991

Index